JAPAN

THE BASICS

Japan: The Basics is an engaging introduction to the culture, society and global positioning of Japan. Taking a fresh look at stereotypes associated with Japan, it provides a well-rounded introduction to a constantly evolving country. It addresses such questions as:

- How do we go about studying Japan?
- What are the connections between popular culture and wider Japanese society?
- How are core values about identity formed and what are their implications?
- How does Japan react to natural and man–made disasters?
- How does nature influence Japanese attitudes to the environment?

With exercises and discussion points throughout and suggestions for further reading, *Japan: The Basics* is an ideal starting point for all those studying Japan in its global, cultural context.

Christopher P. Hood is a Reader in Japanese Studies at Cardiff University, UK. He is the author of *Dealing with Disaster in Japan: Responses to the Flight JL123 Crash* (2011) and *Shinkansen: From Bullet Train to Symbol of Modern Japan* (2006), also published by Routledge.

The Basics

ACTING
BELLA MERLIN

AMERICAN PHILOSOPHY
NANCY STANLICK

ANCIENT NEAR EAST
DANIEL C. SNELL

ANTHROPOLOGY
PETER METCALF

ARCHAEOLOGY (SECOND EDITION)
CLIVE GAMBLE

ART HISTORY
GRANT POOKE AND DIANA NEWALL

ARTIFICIAL INTELLIGENCE
KEVIN WARWICK

THE BIBLE
JOHN BARTON

BIOETHICS
ALASTAIR V. CAMPBELL

BUDDHISM
CATHY CANTWELL

THE CITY
KEVIN ARCHER

CONTEMPORARY LITERATURE
SUMAN GUPTA

CRIMINAL LAW
JONATHAN HERRING

CRIMINOLOGY (SECOND EDITION)
SANDRA WALKLATE

DANCE STUDIES
JO BUTTERWORTH

EASTERN PHILOSOPHY
VICTORIA S. HARRISON

ECONOMICS (SECOND EDITION)
TONY CLEAVER

EDUCATION
KAY WOOD

ENERGY
MICHAEL SCHOBERT

EUROPEAN UNION (SECOND EDITION)
ALEX WARLEIGH-LACK

EVOLUTION
SHERRIE LYONS

FILM STUDIES (SECOND EDITION)
AMY VILLAREJO

FINANCE (SECOND EDITION)
ERIK BANKS

FREE WILL
MEGHAN GRIFFITH

GENDER
HILARY LIPS

GLOBAL MIGRATION
BERNADETTE HANLON AND
THOMAS VICINO

HUMAN GENETICS
RICKI LEWIS

HUMAN GEOGRAPHY
ANDREW JONES

INTERNATIONAL RELATIONS
PETER SUTCH AND JUANITA ELIAS

ISLAM (SECOND EDITION)
COLIN TURNER

JAPAN
THE BASICS

Christopher P. Hood

Routledge
Taylor & Francis Group

LONDON AND NEW YORK

First published 2015
by Routledge
2 Park Square, Milton Park, Abingdon, Oxon OX14 4RN

and by Routledge
711 Third Avenue, New York, NY 10017

Routledge is an imprint of the Taylor & Francis Group, an informa business

British Library Cataloguing in Publication Data
A catalogue record for this book is available from the British Library

Library of Congress Cataloging in Publication Data
Hood, Christopher P. (Christopher Philip), 1971–
  Japan: the basics/Christopher P. Hood.
  pages cm. – (The basics)
  Includes bibliographical references and index.
  1. Japan. I. Title.
  DS806.H66 2015
  952 – dc23
  2014018256

ISBN: 978-0-415-62972-0 (hbk)
ISBN: 978-0-415-62971-3 (pbk)
ISBN: 978-1-315-74568-8 (ebk)

Typeset in Bembo and Scala Sans
by Florence Production Ltd, Stoodleigh, Devon, UK

Printed and bound in Great Britain by
TJ International Ltd, Padstow, Cornwall

To Man Yee, Miella and Monty

and

to the fellow academics and students who inspire me to keep questioning and to try to find answers to the questions

CONTENTS

CONTENTS

ILLUSTRATIONS

FIGURES

Full-size colour versions of the photographs taken by the author can be seen at: www.hood-online.co.uk/japan-the-basics/

TABLES

NOTES ON STYLE

The revised Hepburn Romanisation system is used for Japanese words. An apostrophe is used between combinations 'n' and 'yo', for example, to distinguish between the sounds 'n'yo' and 'nyo'. Macrons are used as appropriate on Japanese words. Macrons denote long vowel sounds and are twice the length of a short vowel in pronunciation. Macrons have been added as appropriate to words in quotations where they were omitted in the original.

All personal names are written in the order given name-family name.

Place names are given in their local spelling (e.g. Napoli rather than Naples).

Dates, when abbreviated, are written according to the ISO 8601 international standard (which is similar to the Japanese system). For example, 12 August 1985 becomes 1985-08-12.

Where translations have not been attributed to other sources, they are my own.

British English spelling is used except when citing a proper name that uses American English spelling. Citations have been altered to be consistent with this where necessary. The universal numbering system (adopted officially in 1974) is used (i.e. 1 billion = 1,000,000,000 and 1 trillion = 1,000,000,000,000).

Metric (SI) measurements are used throughout the text except where discussing laws that use other measurements, for example.

Due to fluctuations in exchange rates, conversions are not used.

ACKNOWLEDGEMENTS

This book is in many ways a culmination of all of my 37 visits to Japan to date rather than the result of a single project or one fieldwork trip. What is contained within this book is born from over 25 years of studying the country and the language. It has been shaped by my own studies and by hearing the work of other academics at conferences and reading their books, chapters and articles. It is also inspired by the teaching that I have been doing for about 20 years. Consequently, I would like to acknowledge all of those that have supported me and inspired me over the years. It would be difficult to mention all of those who deserve credit in this respect. Instead, I would like to just give a special mention to some of those who have played a particularly significant role.

First and foremost, I would like to acknowledge the support and encouragement of my family. While my wife and children share an interest in Japan, they have been less enthusiastic about some of the hours required to get the book written, let alone when I have made my own trips to Japan, so their patience has been much appreciated. I would also like to thank the support of my parents, my sister Maz, whose own interest in Japan may have helped lead me to start this journey of discovery, and my uncle Robin.

Then there are my many friends who have encouraged me to keep going, and in relation to this book, particularly my Japanese friends who have also provided places to stay and/or insights into Japan: the Gotoh family, Yoshi and Kimiko Tanabe, Suguru Funatsu, Masaaki Yamada, Ryō Suzuki, Kosuke Nakao, Yumi Katayama and the rest of the Concord College gang.

It would be impossible to name here all of the other academics who have inspired and helped me develop my understanding of Japan over the years. Many of them appear in references throughout the book, but I would like to particularly thank Graham Healey, Joy Hendry, Glenn Hook, Earl Kinmonth, Jeff Kingston, Helen Macnaughtan, Peter Matanle, Tom McAuley and Arthur Stockwin.

We never stop learning about Japan. But at the same time, I am teaching about Japan. Much is said about 'research-led teaching', but it is important not to overlook the significance of 'teaching-led research'. The views, interests and questions of students kindle much of my passion to learn and teach more about Japan. In many ways, it is the experiences of interacting with my students that helped to shape this book.

Although this book is the result of many years of visits to Japan, a trip in 2013 was instrumental in pulling many of the ideas together, and I would like to thank here the Great Britain Sasakawa Foundation and its Chief Executive, Stephen McEnally, for supporting it.

Although most of the pictures in this book are my own work, the image of Hokusai's *Beneath a Wave off Kanagawa* was provided by the Yale University Art Gallery, and I would like to thank them for this. I would also like to thank JR East, Sanrio Entertainment and Cateriam Cat Café in Shimo-Kitazawa for allowing me to include pictures taken in their facilities.

Finally, I would like to thank Japan and the Japanese people for being such an interesting focus for an inquisitive mind.

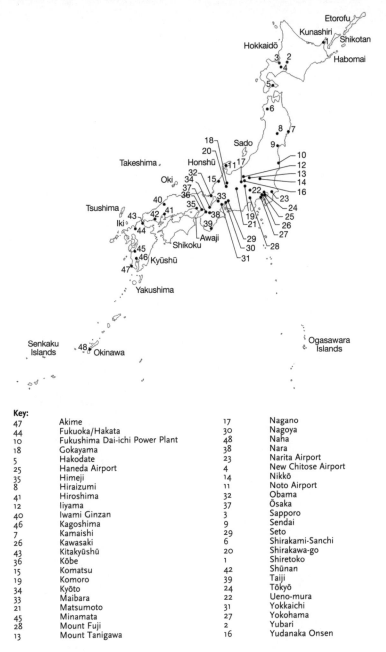

Figure 0.1 Map of Japan

STUDYING JAPAN

Today, in these exotic streets, the old and the new mingle so well that one seems to set off the other.

(Hearn 2005: locations 137–9)

Japan is real. But does our understanding of Japan match with the reality of Japan today? For many who will read this book, Japan is a distant land. Even in a world connected by jet planes, getting to Japan can still take considerable time. Even from the capitals of some of its closest neighbours, the flight to Tōkyō can take in excess of two hours, while from Europe, North America and Australasia it takes about half a day. Perhaps due to this distance, we assume that where we are going to will be different to what we have left behind; the longer the journey, the greater the differences. But perhaps this logic leads us to look for the differences at the expense of seeing the similarities. Do we look at Japan with our own eyes or are we destined to seek out and replicate the observations that others have made for generations before us? The opening quotation to this chapter is one that probably strikes a chord with anyone who reads this book. Yet it was written by a visitor to Japan towards the end of the nineteenth century during the Meiji period (1868–1912).

But Japan is not static. Things do change; politicians, and in recent years prime ministers in particular, come and go; there seems to be a never-ending conveyer belt of new fresh faces coming to the music scene; and in international relations there can be disputes and events that can have a seemingly significant impact beyond the political and diplomatic levels. Such seemingly significant events or people are a reflection of something much deeper and core within Japan. Understanding these aspects of Japan, which themselves may change, albeit at a slower rate, is a key foundation upon which studies of more specific issues can be developed.

Another important aspect about understanding Japan, and almost any aspect of it, is having a holistic approach to it. Just as the separate parts of the body are connected, so the operations of a country are. For example, in the past decade we have seen a large increase in the number of people interested in Japan due to a love of *manga*, *anime*, Japanese movies, television dramas or music. Naturally, each of these outputs can reflect a number of aspects of Japanese society. If we consider a *manga*, while its storyline may be fictitious, depending on the genre, if the 'Japanese content' is to be fully understood and appreciated it may well include contents that require a knowledge of a variety of themes, including the education system, the way the language operates and the way Japanese cities are laid out. But in understanding Japan, there is more to it than merely the content of the *manga* itself. That the particular *manga* was published, marketed and tied in with other products relates to how business operates in Japan. So anything 'Japanese' can be used to help us understand a variety of aspects of Japan and Japanese society. What we mean by 'Japanese' is something that we will need to consider later in the book.

THE START OF THE JOURNEY

At this point, it is worth pointing out some of the assumptions upon which this book is based. The first of these is that you are near the start of your quest to learn more about Japan. Although it is likely that many readers are either nearing the end of secondary school or starting university and may be about to or are just embarking upon studies about Japan at university as part of their degree, the book will be just as relevant for those who are coming to the subject from a very different background.

Whatever your background, the assumption is that you want to learn about Japan and that you are going to dedicate time and energy beyond the reading of this book to do that. This book will aid you as you start out in this process, helping you to develop skills and an attitude to think for yourself about how Japan works.

This book will also point out some of the other materials available on the subject so that you can read about it further. Most academic books are around 100,000 words long. But books in *The Basics* series are much shorter and concentrate on introducing key issues as a springboard for further study, for example by reading some of the materials that you will see in references throughout the book. Many academics in Japanese studies focus their attention on writing books (including chapters in edited collections – where it may not always be obvious from the title of the book that there is a chapter of relevance to a topic you may be researching). You need to keep in mind publication times. It will typically take about nine months for a book to be published after the script is submitted. The research itself is likely to have stopped some months before the manuscript is sent in, so it is not uncommon for the research to be a year old by the time it is published. This can be a lot shorter when dealing with articles in practitioner, non-refereed journals, or when just placed on a website. But some of these will not have gone through the same review process, so you may have to be more careful about how you treat the contents. Remember that things change from year to year, and you should look to check what the latest data reveal and then consider why the situation may have changed alongside what academics and others have already written on the subject. For this book, I have tried to focus on providing English language sources as I have assumed that as a new student to Japanese studies, your use of the Japanese language is limited.

Developing a deep understanding of Japan is not a quick process. It may take years of additional reading of books and articles, personal visits to Japan, and viewing of media. But the journey of discovery is likely to be an exciting one and rewarding in many different ways. For it is likely that along the way, you will discover more about yourself, as well as Japan.

Whatever your background, you already know things about Japan. One of the aims of this book is to act as a bridge between that knowledge and the academic texts. Even if you think that you do not know much about Japan, in reality it is likely that you have been exposed to Japan in a variety of forms throughout your life. This book will help you to draw upon this knowledge and then develop it by encouraging you on to further study of Japan. In other words, this book will provide the foundations and means to think about how to use links to help you go on to become an expert in Japan. To help achieve the aims of the book, there will be a number of exercises to complete. These exercises will help you to explore the knowledge you already have and to gain additional awareness about the country. While in some cases there are correct answers, in some cases there will not be. Even where correct answers exist, I have not provided an answer section in this book as I want to encourage you to go and research the answers yourself. I would like you to complete the first of these, Exercise 1.1, now.

EXERCISE 1.1

For five minutes, sit in silence with your eyes shut. During that time, I want you to just focus on the word 'Japan' and then see what images are conjured up in your mind. At the end of the five minutes, write down what images came to mind. Refer back to this list as you read through the book and do the exercises in each chapter.

WHAT TO STUDY?

Let us consider the contents of the list that you compiled as part of Exercise 1.1. Let us call each of these items a symbol of Japan. For the purpose of this book, you do not need to have a particular understanding of symbols or their study, semiotics; for that, there is another book in *The Basics* series, *Semiotics: The Basics* (Chandler 2007). I would like to explore and develop your understanding of Japan based upon your list of symbols. The problem with doing this is that I cannot see your list. Instead, I will share some of my symbols of Japan. I hope that I will address some of those that you have listed, but ideally I will not deal with many of them. I hope that the book will encourage you to think about how you would deal with the remaining symbols on your list yourself, while also researching the symbols that I have addressed further, as well as other questions about Japan that you may already have or gain as a result of your studies and experiences of Japan.

Before we move on to discuss how we will study Japan, we need to keep in mind some of the issues of using symbols to study Japan. As you will probably be aware from your own list, there are many different types of symbols. What concerns us here are 'public symbols' (Hendry 1999: 82), that is the ones, whether they be events, people or things, that are in the public domain and are 'typical' or 'natural'. Indeed, such symbols may be so natural that 'it is often the case that people within one society remain blissfully unaware of the relativity of their symbols' (Hendry 1999: 83).

In relation to studying symbols and Japan, it is natural to refer to Roland Barthes' *Empire of Signs*. His study is of 'Japan', but it is not the 'real' Japan, for Barthes was describing 'a fictive nation . . . so as to compromise no real country' (Barthes 1983: 3). Despite this caveat, what is described within is recognisable as being the country that Barthes had visited, without any linguistic knowledge of the Japanese language, in 1966. So why mention his study? There are two reasons. First, his study offers hope. It is possible to study and begin to comprehend Japan with the simplest of skills: a desire to learn, an ability to observe and an enquiring mind. Knowledge of the Japanese language is not essential, but can be beneficial, in taking steps to understand Japan, as we will discuss further below. Second, Barthes' study highlights how we can begin to understand a nation by looking at certain 'symbols' and trying to comprehend them.

A problem of symbols, and this is a key point to be aware of in terms of our study of Japan, is that we must be careful not to project our own ideas and interpretations on to what it is we are studying. To understand this point, you may find it helpful to watch the lecture delivered by Tom Hanks' character during the opening minutes of the film *The Da Vinci Code* (Ron Howard, 2006), where he illustrates how various symbols have very opposing interpretations depending on your background. Indeed,

Cohen (1986: 7) questions whether the symbols are more significant for us rather than the people we are studying.

A further problem with trying to draw conclusions about a country or culture as a whole from a single event, for example, is that thought needs to be given as to whether what we are witnessing is truly typical or not. There is also a danger that we may overanalyse. Consider for a moment the firework displays and bonfires around Britain every year on 5 November. These are symbolic of a nation's desire to remember the events when Guy Fawkes and his comrades attempted to blow up the Houses of Parliament. In other words, it is a symbolic display that Britain does not give in to terrorists. But is this association made by most people taking part in the events, or is the priority the fun and entertainment? We will be returning to a discussion of these issues in Chapter 5.

LANGUAGE

As noted, while it may be possible to study Japan to some degree without knowledge of the language, some knowledge can be highly beneficial. A balance is needed. Without the knowledge, you are reliant upon the translations and interpretations of others. Without the help of others, you are reliant upon ensuring your own knowledge is better than their ability to translate and interpret. Given that in a dictionary there may be a number of suggested translations for each word, each with their own nuance, it is likely that the process of learning a language to a stage whereby you can use it without any helpers will be a long one. By their very nature, translations are a compromise.

Language reflects the cultural workings of the group that use the language. Without an understanding of how that culture operates, the words will lose some of their inherent meaning. It is for this reason that good translations should include annotations from the translators to help explain the context and cultural-specific dimensions to the reader. Let me give an example to illustrate this. Imagine a film in which somebody sneezes and a person reacts to this. As the lips are seen to move, so a translation will be needed. If in Britain, the person speaking is likely to say 'Bless you', whereas in Japan they would most probably say '*samui desu ka*'. These are perfectly acceptable translations of each other in this context. They both reflect what would be said in such a situation. However, the literal translation of the Japanese phrase is 'Are you cold?' and shows that even in such a mundane situation, what is said from one culture to another can vary greatly.

This book cannot teach you Japanese, but having some understanding of the way in which the language works will be beneficial. The most important fact to be aware of is that the language is phonetic – it is made up of a combination of around 46 different sounds, revolving around five basic vowel sounds. When it comes to writing Japanese, there are four ways in which it may be written. It can be written using Romanised letters (referred to as *Rōmaji*). The problem with using this system is that there is a tendency for those of us who use Romanised scripts for our own languages to ignore Japanese phonetics and pronounce words in the way that a similarly written word would be in our own language. Although there are generally accepted ways of how Japanese should be Romanised, with the revised Hepburn system being the most widely used, it is not uncommon to come across variations, particularly used by many Japanese themselves, and so be careful before concluding one system is 'right' or 'better' than others. Most of the time, Japanese is not written using *Rōmaji*, but through a combination of *kanji*, *hiragana* and *katakana*. *Kanji* are the Chinese characters used for particular words, and each character carries its own meaning. Unlike Chinese, in Japanese most *kanji* have more than one way that they may be pronounced depending on the context. *Hiragana* and *katakana* are based upon the Japanese phonetic alphabet, and the characters carry no meaning in themselves. *Hiragana* is the most commonly used, with *katakana* typically being used for foreign words, onomatopoeia and to give emphasis to words.

Japanese sentences typically follow the pattern of subject–object–verb. However, many sentences will have no subject, with the subject carrying over from the previous sentence. There is no singular or plural. Nouns do not have gender. There are limited tenses for verbs. Pronouns are rarely used. On the face of it, Japanese grammar may seem relatively straightforward when compared to many European languages. One of the greatest challenges comes from the ambiguity that can exist, particularly if a sentence is taken out of context. The suffix 'san' can mean Mr, Miss or Mrs, and it is possible that in a book, the gender of the person may only become clear after some pages, meaning that any translations into English with the incorrect pronoun would need to be corrected. Of course, such cases are rare as normally a means is found to provide clarity to avoid confusion. So rather than say a sentence that could lead to uncertainty as to whether there is a single pencil on a table or many pencils on a table, the Japanese sentence is likely to include precise information or at least an estimate to the number of pencils on the table.

While nouns in Japanese have no gender, the way in which the language is used typically varies depending on whether the person is male or female. There are certain words, particularly when referring to oneself, that are only used by males or females. Similarly, there are different words used depending on the status of the people interacting. Having an awareness of this can be useful when considering the statement being made by a female who uses words that would more generally used by males, for example. A simple translation would not highlight this usage of the language, and the point can only be made if your own knowledge of the language is good enough or your helper provides sufficient commentary. A similar problem can arise for male non-Japanese who learn Japanese, as many Japanese teachers are female and imitating their natural tone and vocabulary will lead their Japanese not sounding how many male Japanese would naturally sound.

There are also differences between the spoken and written Japanese language. In terms of the written language, the key point to be aware of is that traditionally, Japanese has been written vertically, starting on the right of the page and proceeding left. Although more and more books, and particularly web pages, are being written from left to right and moving down line by line, vertical writing is still common. In terms of our study of Japan, the way in which the language is written, and so by extension how the Japanese eyes work and render information, may be different to our own. To try to understand this point, compare the two images in Figures 1.1 and 1.2. Looking at Figure 1.1, for those used to reading from left to right it is the wave that dominates the image. However, if you want to understand how

Figure 1.1 Beneath a Wave off Kanagawa

Source: Based on an image provided by the Yale University Art Gallery.

Figure 1.2 Beneath a Wave off Kanagawa (reversed)

Source: Based on an image provided by the Yale University Art Gallery.

many Japanese would comprehend the picture, we need to flip it by 180°. Having done this, one can see that it is Mount Fuji that appears to be the key component of the image. One has to keep such differences in mind when we try to interpret the visuals of Japan; we need to be careful to look as a local would, and not with our own eyes. Although often known as 'The Great Wave', the picture is part of Hokusai's collection of 36 images of Mount Fuji, and its title *Beneath a Wave off Kanagawa* reflects this Fuji-centric focus.

Being aware that many Japanese may see things differently to yourself is important when it comes to how you analyse web pages, for example. While you may find that a Japanese web page may appear cluttered, for Japanese people used to reading books and newspapers in a particular layout and format, the design may appear more appealing.

Throughout this book, you will see that there are a number of photographs. You should treat each of these as an exercise. While the text relating to the photographs may give some indication of the issues relating to each photograph's contents, you should take some time to explore the photographs and ask yourself questions such as what the image teaches us about Japan, what is missing from the image that you may have expected and what other interpretations could be made of what is depicted in the photographs.

STEREOTYPES AND CONTEXT

Let us return to the quotation that opened this chapter. It was suggested that those words would resonate with many who visit Japan today. But I would also suggest that they could be applied to most countries around the world. In relation to this, I would like you do the next exercise.

The first of these quotations comes again from Hearn's diary of a visit to Japan in the Meiji period, while the second is from Barthes, who has also been introduced in this chapter. The other statements are by different people in their personal statements of applications to study Japanese at university. As can be seen, there are certain common themes that have echoed throughout time in our descriptions of Japan. Seemingly, not much has changed

EXERCISE 1.2

Read and analyse the following statements. In particular, consider to what degree you think the statements could be applied to countries and cultures other than Japan. How do the statements relate to your list of symbols? To what degree do you think the statements are valid?

1 'Their simple politeness is not an art; their goodness is absolutely unconscious goodness; both come straight from the heart' (Hearn 2005: locations 1362–3).

2 'The Japanese picturesque is indifferent to us, for it is detached from what constitutes the very speciality of Japan, which is its modernity' (Barthes 1983: 79).

3 'The fascinating combination of tradition and modernity so typical for Japan'.

4 'Even though the Japanese way of life has changed significantly since WWII, it still remains a subject of great curiosity for many'.

5 'Japan is a country full of diversity and surprises'.

6 'Japan is "a country that has seemed in an almost mythical far east" for me'.

7 'Japanese culture is truly remarkable and holds an intense fascination for me'.

8 'Their etiquette was nothing I have ever experienced before – bowing ... showing respect and honour'.

in over 100 years. Perhaps this is not surprising. For as Buruma (2001: ix) notes, 'It is hard to avoid the clichés about Japan, because both Japanese and foreigners seem to feel most comfortable with them'. Furthermore, Littlewood states that:

> One by one, the time-honoured images turn out to be true. But in doing so, they obscure all the other things that are true – which is why they are so dangerous. They teach us what to look for, and that is what we find; everything else becomes a background blur. We are left with a reality selected for us by our stereotypes.
>
> (Littlewood 1996: xiii)

But there are times when cultures come to replicate stereotypes. In her study of *nisei* (second-generation Japanese Americans) predominantly from Hawai'i who worked as Pan Am stewardesses and how they were employed as they may have had the qualities that some passengers were thought to desire, Yano (2011: 105) points out that 'Hearing a stereotype "over and over" is exactly where racial and cultural reputations lie – in the self-prophesying realm of expectations'.

Of course, stereotypes are, or at least were, based on some sort of reality. They do not necessarily represent what the majority do (or did), but what a significant number of people were thought to do. That it is mentioned is likely to be a reflection of behaviour that is in some way different to our own society. In that respect, we need to keep in mind that many may 'normalise' their own behaviour and think that what they do and think is similar to the general population, and so presumed differences in another society may overlook similarities around them. The danger is that while the stereotype may have been merely an oversimplification and generalisation that was developed to highlight a perceived difference from one's own society, due to changes over time it may now not reflect a norm at all.

Our concern here is not so much when, how and why certain stereotypes relating to Japan were created, but the degree to which they continue to exist and how we can go about studying Japan without slipping into the trap of finding and reinforcing stereotypes and clichés that do not accurately reflect the reality of Japan today. Let us consider just one of the phrases in Exercise 1.2 – the third one. Yes, Japan is a country of contrasts. By the new futuristic skyscrapers, there may be old houses, temples or shrines (see Figure 1.3) – in a way that echoes the sentiment of the quotation that opened this chapter. But I would suggest that Japan is not unusual in having such contrasts existing side by side. London's newest skyscrapers tower over terraced housing dating back much further than their Japanese counterparts and its churches may be many hundreds of years old. I expect you could find an equivalent in your closest city.

So why do we continue to see stereotypes being used so much? The answer to this may lie in our propensity to rely upon descriptions that others have used before us. When asking about

Figure 1.3 Modern and traditional side by side. A variety of trains passing inbetween the skyscrapers and a shrine in Tōkyō.

the experience of visiting Japan, an individual is not expecting a long, detailed answer. The respondent knows this and so instinctively will tend to look for an anchor point that helps the other person connect with the answer. These anchors tend to be heavily reliant upon stereotypes and clichés. Although such stereotypes and clichés may change over time, they tend to be a conservative force and remain used by many – even if they do not reflect the norm. Indeed, they may never have reflected the norm at all, but may have been based upon a desire to highlight a difference with one's own culture and society. Other times, they may be a reflection of the fact that we do not look at our own society with the same attention as we do a place that we visit as strangers. Of course, we as individuals are not the only ones that rely upon stereotypes. They are often found in TV programmes, movies and the media. We will be looking at some of these in relation to Japan throughout the book. For starters, please now complete Exercise 1.3.

EXERCISE 1.3

Watch the episode of *The Simpsons* called '30 Minutes over Tokyo' (Season 10, Episode 23). If you cannot find this episode, then try to watch a movie set in Japan, such as *Lost in Translation* (Sofia Coppola, 2003). As you watch, keep a list of the various stereotypes that you see. Does anything about them offend you? If so, why?

As suggested above, it is sometimes not only outsiders that rely upon certain symbols and stereotypes in describing a country. Thinking about your symbols from Exercise 1.1, did you include something related to *manga*, *anime* and other 'soft cultural exports' such as Hello Kitty? In recent years, it has been 'soft cultural exports', as opposed to the exports of tangible items such as cars and electronics, which you may have also listed, that have been sowing the seeds of interest in Japan (and people's assumptions about Japan) for more and more people around the world. Indeed, so prevalent has this become that the Japanese government itself has sought to capitalise upon it by promoting tourism to the country, for example under the banner of 'Cool Japan'.

So far in this book, we have discussed symbols and stereotypes. Another term that we have used is culture. But what exactly do we mean by culture, and in this context Japanese culture? At its simplest level, culture is probably best understood as what underpins the actions of a group or society. One of the first definitions of culture was by Edward Tyler (1873: 1), who suggested that a 'Culture or civilization, taken in its wide ethnographic sense, is that complex whole which includes knowledge, belief, art, morals, law, custom, and any other capabilities and habits acquired by man as a member of society'. But this is by no means the only definition, and for the purpose of this book and your studies of Japan you need to be aware that the term itself can be somewhat problematic. You may find it useful to read another book in *The Basics* series, *Anthropology: The Basics* (Metcalf 2005), to learn more about this. Here, the issue I would like you to keep in mind is that while we may speak of 'Japanese culture', within Japan there are many other cultures depending on the context. For example, in general people in Tōkyō may do some things in a way that are different to people in Ōsaka. So there may be a 'Tōkyō culture' and also an 'Ōsaka culture'. But even within Tōkyō, not all people will necessarily act according to the expectations of 'Tōkyō culture', perhaps due to conforming to another 'culture' that is of greater significance to them. Across the country, there may be aspects of commonality between many of these cultures. This may be the basis of what we could call 'Japanese culture'. The key point, though, is that differences exist, and keeping this in mind is central to avoiding overusing stereotypes and clichés.

What we need to try to avoid are generalisations. As Kinmonth points out:

One way of testing the acceptability of cultural generalizations about Japan and the Japanese that I suggest to students is take an assertion about 'Japanese' and substitute Jews for Japanese, or Blacks for Japanese, or Hispanics for Japanese, or 'Gypsies' for Japanese, or Catholics for Japanese or any minority for Japanese. Whether the generalization is something that might or might not be said about the substitute group is irrelevant. One issue is tone. If the result is cringe inducing when targeted at Jews, ask yourself why it is acceptable to make the same generalization about Japanese. Another, is breadth. If the result sounds overly broad when made about Cubans, for example, ask yourself why it is acceptable to make the same generalization about Japanese. A third test is political correctness. Make the substitution. If you start to think, 'If I said something like that about Blacks, people would be on my case calling me a racist', then ask yourself why it is acceptable to say the same thing about Japanese.

(Kinmonth 2014)

A natural part of studying Japan is to put research into context by providing an international comparison. But we need to be careful in making international comparisons and how we draw conclusions from them. Remember the need for a holistic approach. If Japan scores better in international educational tests, this does not necessarily mean that it would be appropriate to adopt Japanese educational methods into another country, for Japan's education system is supported by a number of other features of Japanese society including how the family works, moral beliefs and even the operations of the labour market. Having an understanding of these connections and how to find them is the key to becoming a top specialist about Japan. Also, remember if you are to do a thorough international comparison, you will need to do as much reading and researching about each country you are comparing and do not assume you know everything about your own country. It is too easy to normalise and make assumptions about beliefs and behaviour in our own country based upon our own ideas and behaviour.

The issues discussed in relation to international comparisons bring us back to a question that we have so far avoided: why study Japan? There is no single answer to this. A lot depends on who is asking it and on what basis he or she is asking it. There may be lessons that we can learn from Japan and teach others around the world. There may also be things that we can teach Japan based on other knowledge and expertise that we have. There are times when we just need to understand Japan to help for better interaction with Japanese people. For some, perhaps the question as to why study Japan infers whether we should study another country, such as China, rather than Japan. However, most, if not all, countries need graduates with more international knowledge, experience and skills in intercultural communication. Yes, in many countries there may be a need for more people to study China, but there is still a need for more to study Japan too. Whatever the reason to study Japan, one thing that is needed is an open mind and a desire to learn. Believing in a particular set of positivist ways that ultimately all people, societies and cultures will converge and agree on is likely to hinder your ability to objectively study Japan. You have to be prepared to put your personal beliefs to one side and accept that differences exist, even if sometimes you do not like them, and try to come to understand why Japan does what it does in the way that it does.

START WITH THE BASICS

To help ensure that we do not fall into the trap of relying on stereotypes and clichés, a good starting point is to go back to the basics. The first thing to consider is just where is Japan. The answer to this is perhaps not as straightforward as you may think. While it is natural to turn to a map or atlas to check a location, there are many problems with maps. As maps tend to be flat, while the globe is not, distortions of some kind are to be expected. The most commonly used map is the Mercator projection, which exaggerates the size of countries in the northern hemisphere, with the distortion becoming greater the further away from the equator the location is. In the case of Japan, the distortion is not that apparent until you try to compare its size to some northern European countries or countries in the southern hemisphere.

But when dealing with Japan, the problem is not so much where is Japan, but what is Japan. The issue of the territorial disputes and the geographical limitations of Japan's borders is one that we will return to in Chapter 6. But if we look at standard maps of Japan, there are a few things that you need to be aware of. First, is north at the top? Of course, it need not be, but it is usual for maps to have the lines of longitude being largely parallel to the sides of the map or page of the atlas. Due to Japan's length and shape, however, you may come across maps that do not adhere to this convention, and this can somewhat distort our perception of where places are in relation to others. Second, where are Hokkaidō and Okinawa? Sometimes, in an attempt to fit the country on one page, Hokkaidō is moved to an inset. The Okinawa chain is similarly often moved to an inset or it may not be included at all. Any changes such as this can alter our perception and understanding of just how far these islands are from the rest of Japan.

Japan is often referred to as being made up of four islands. Indeed, the Hollywood movie *The Last Samurai* (Edward Zwick, 2003) even suggests that these were the original four islands as according to Shintō legend. In fact, according to Shintō, as presented in the book *Kojiki* written in 712, there were *eight* islands created: Awaji, Honshū, Shikoku, Kyūshū, Oki, Tsushima, Iki and Sado. Hokkaidō and Okinawa did not become part of Japan until the nineteenth century. But of course, even a cursory study of a map of Japan reveals that the country is in fact made up of many hundreds of islands.

It is important to familiarise ourselves with the countries we study. We should have an awareness of certain basic facts, and I would encourage you to do Exercise 1.4 at this point.

EXERCISE 1.4

Answer the following questions. Try to do this without using any reference materials first and then check your answers afterwards.

1   What is the name of the capital city?
2   How many constituent prefectures (equivalent to counties in the UK or states in the USA, for example) are there and what is each of them called?
3   What is the name of the tallest mountain and how high is it?
4   What is the name of the longest river and how long is it?
5   What are the names of the 10 largest cities?
6   What are the names of the monarch/president and the prime minister?

Having completed this exercise for Japan, try doing the same for your own country without using any reference materials – you may be shocked to discover how little you know about your own country!

As well as being aware of some of the basic facts about Japan, the country, there are some other basic cultural points that are worth keeping in mind.

The first of these relates to dates. Although the Gregorian calendar is commonly used in Japan, for many official documents in particular, the Japanese calendar based on the reign of the emperor is used. Under this system, when there is a new emperor, a new name for that era will be decided upon and used in conjunction with the length of the reign. Should there be a change in emperor in December, the whole of that year will be renamed as being the first year of the new era. The current era is called Heisei and it started in 1989 – but remember that if you are trying to calculate the current year, you have to subtract 1988, as otherwise 1989 would be Heisei 0 rather than Heisei 1. Many Japanese also use the Chinese signs of the zodiac, but the change happens on 1 January rather than with the start of the Chinese New Year, which tends to be in February (so somebody whose birthday is in February, for example, may find that they have different signs of the zodiac depending on whether they are speaking to a Chinese or Japanese person). Although the year starts on 1 January in Japan, the academic and fiscal years start on 1 April. Some of the symbolic reasons for this and its implications will be discussed in Chapter 7. In Japan, dates are written in the order year-month-day, which, as it happens, is also how all dates on the Internet are also supposed to be written according to the ISO 8601 international standard.

By now, you will have noticed that Tōkyō has been written with small lines, called macrons, on the o's. Macrons indicate that the vowel length should be doubled. In many publications, they are not included. In some, they are omitted from commonly used place names, for example. When you read anything, you should check the 'Notes on style' of that publication to see what convention they are using so that you can help avoid possible confusion about whether two places in two different publications, one with macrons and one without, are actually the same place or not. When it comes to your own work, unless you are presented with a style sheet to conform to, I suggest that you take some time to think about what conventions you would like to use and make it clear to the reader in your own 'Notes on style' section. The convention of not putting macrons on common place names, for example, seems to be a bizarre halfway house between being technically correct and not using macrons at all. I would always recommend that you are consistent and either always use them on all words, or do not use them at all.

We need to keep in mind the conventions that our readers will be used to. After all, in English we commonly change place names; for example, Firenze becomes Florence, Warsawa becomes Warsaw and Caerdydd becomes Cardiff. Perhaps when characters that we do not use in our own alphabet are in the original, the change is more understandable; for example, København becoming Copenhagen. But we need to be mindful of the message sent out by the choice of word; for example, using Kiev rather than Kyiv would indicate sympathy to the Russian spelling rather than the Ukrainian, using Peking rather than Beijing would indicate a preference to use Cantonese rather than Mandarin, and Mount Everest, although perhaps the most well-known used term in English, ignores the local names, Chomolungma in Tibetan and Sagarmāthā in Nepalese. Being aware of the local names can be useful when studying Japanese, as generally Japanese will use the local name as the basis for writing it in the phonetic *katakana* script rather than how the place may be known in English. Of course, this can lead to separate issues where there are variations over the pronunciation of the place – such as Shrewsbury in England, and remember the 's' of Paris is not pronounced in French. Perhaps a more complicated issue is when you deal with trademarks and such like. When talking about the Disneyland resort in Japan, should it be Tōkyō Disneyland, Tokyo Disneyland or Tōkyō Dizunīrando? Similarly, some Japanese use an 'h' on the end of their name to denote the long vowel when not using macrons. So should we stick to the convention of macrons in the case of the name Gotō, for example, or leave it as Gotoh, and so treating the name as though it were a trademark?

In relation to Japan, there are some other name issues to be aware of. Let us first consider the name of the country. In Japanese, it is known as Nippon or Nihon. These are the two alternative readings for how the name is written in *kanji*: 日本. I suspect you already know that this means 'land of the rising sun'. Actually, this is not strictly accurate. The first character does mean sun (or day), but the second means the source (and can also mean 'book'). But if standing on the east coast of Japan, the sun is not rising in Japan, but out somewhere in the Pacific – the USA would be a more appropriate country to refer to as the land of the rising sun from the Japanese perspective. It is from the Chinese perspective that the sun rises in Japan, and that is where the name comes from. There was originally another word for the country: Yamato (大和). 'Japan' is based on the Cantonese pronunciation of the word. Today in Japan, you will find that Mandarin announcements on trains, for example, will give the Mandarin pronunciation for the *kanji* of place names in Japan, which can cause some confusion if you try talking to a Chinese person about a particular city, shrine or temple!

Two towns in Japan have had interesting experiences relating to names in recent years. Maibara station in central Japan was for a long time an important intersection, allowing passengers to transfer between lines running along the east and west coasts of Honshū. The name of the station was derived from the standard reading of the *kanji* 米原. However, the station name was an anomaly as the town in which it was located was actually called Maihara. In 2005, as part of a process of municipal mergers (see Chapter 3), Maihara town merged with Santō and Ibuki towns to create a new city. The name that was chosen was Maibara. In a different sort of name linkage, in 2008 a small city in Fukui prefecture seemingly threw its support behind one of the two US presidential candidates as they shared the same name: Obama. When Barack Obama was sworn in as president in 2009, Obama in Japan held a celebration in his honour (NBC 2009) and the president subsequently referred to the link in a speech he made during a visit to Japan (The White House 2009). Before leaving the subject of place names and *kanji*, it is worth noting that although the United Kingdom is commonly referred to as *Igirisu* in Japanese, it may also be written using the *kanji* 英国 (*Eikoku*). You may find that some Japanese will translate both *Igirisu* and *Eikoku* as England rather than the United Kingdom. The irony is that the *kanji* comes from the first character being pronounced 'ying' in Cantonese (the second character means country or land) and so is an approximation to the sound 'Eng' of 'England'! For the USA, the standard way of writing it in *kanji* in Japan and China is different (米国/美国), although in Japanese it is often referred to by the *katakana Amerika*.

When it comes to personal names, the main thing to be aware of is that it is normal to order their names with surname followed by personal name. For example, in the case of Tanaka Tarō, the surname is Tanaka. How should we order Japanese names in English? How should we order our own name in Japanese? Although most Japanese are aware that names are done in a different order in English, it can still lead to confusion – as can be seen sometimes when Japanese names are written on Facebook where the individual him or herself has seemingly mixed up his or her given name and surname. Many Japanese studies publications written in English will present Japanese names in 'the Japanese order', but you should double-check the style sheet.

Finally in this section, let us consider some numbering issues. The Japanese currency is the yen (¥). This is the currency that would be used in shops in Japan. And yet it is not uncommon to read publications talking about Japanese customers spending X amount of dollars for a car, for example. They did not. They bought the car in yen. The problem with giving the figure in dollars is that it does not take account of the huge currency fluctuations that can happen, as we will discuss further in Chapter 2. You should always give the yen figure. If you want to additionally give a conversion, by all means do so, but make sure you note what rate you were using. Also, please note that Japan uses the metric measuring system, so you will need to get a feel for what a kilometre, kilogram and Celsius are if you are used to using the imperial system.

SUMMARY

The book does not focus specifically on particular current issues as Japan is in a constant state of flux. What seems like a major issue now may not even be remembered in a few years' time. What is important is to provide the skills and knowledge of fundamental elements of Japan, the basics, so that it becomes possible to understand and analyse any event or action by oneself.

The purpose of the book is not to dwell on a small handful of topics and provide in-depth analysis on each. Think of it more like a journey around Japan. Just as the scenery keeps changing as you look out of the window, so the topics will change, from paragraph to paragraph, from section to section and from chapter to chapter. The book will provide a flavour of what Japan is like. But in the end, you need to get out and do your own exploring. Consequently, this book does not provide all the answers. It will help open your mind to how to study Japan. It will raise additional questions – sometimes directly, other times you may think of your own questions. The hope is this will inspire you to do further research of your own about Japan.

The book encourages you to see how subjects are interrelated and to take a holistic approach to studying different aspects of Japan. Because of this approach, it is inevitable that we will sometimes need to return to certain subjects in different chapters. As a result of developing a well-rounded understanding of Japan, as you continue on with your studies of Japan you will be able to formulate why something happens in the way that it does, even if you have not studied that aspect of Japan before, based upon your knowledge of how Japan as a whole operates. This skill development will also enable you to think for yourself about the reliability of media stories relating to Japan, for example, where still too often inaccurate stories are published, as will be discussed throughout the book.

In order to develop a good understanding of Japan, you need to begin with the basics and be aware of some of the key facts and information about the country, its people and its language. You also need to be aware of the problems of being overly reliant upon stereotypes and clichés.

2

DEMOGRAPHIC CHALLENGES

Japan is surreal. When we travel to Japan, no matter how much we try to empty ourselves of preconceptions about what the country is like, we will carry with us a range of images that we expect to see. Many of these images will be the ones that you listed during Exercise 1.1. Perhaps you listed things of natural beauty, such as Mount Fuji, which we will discuss in Chapter 4, or temples and shrines, which we will discuss in Chapter 5. But it is also probable that you have selected images that reflect Japan's urban culture, its bustling way of life and even its use of technology. But while for Exercise 1.1 you were able to list these many different images of Japan, there are times when only a single image can be used. When the director of a film or television programme makes a programme and they need to select an image or scene that can effectively replace the words 'Tōkyō, Japan' on screen or use of a map, they usually do not have the luxury of being able to select multiple images, but need to select one. One of those that has become pervasive is Shibuya's scramble crossing, whereby all the pedestrian lights go green at the same time, allowing for crossing in every direction (see Figure 2.1). In this chapter, we will effectively start by travelling to Shibuya and consider what we can learn about Japan through what we can see in the image of that famous crossing and the area around it.

Figure 2.1 The Shibuya scramble crossing

Whether seen in daylight or at night, there is no doubt that the sight of a mass of people flowing across the pedestrian crossing, surrounded by tall buildings that are covered with bright neon signs and enormous screens, is impressive. Of course, there are equivalents in other cities around the world, whether it be Times Square in New York or Piccadilly Circus in London. But for some reason, it is this crossing rather than any other sight that television and film directors will home in on. Given that many directors like to pay homage to images and films that have influenced them, it is probable that part of the reason for the image's adoption owes much to Ridley Scott's 1982 film *Blade Runner*. Although set in Los Angeles rather than Tōkyō, the images of a futuristic world bear a striking resemblance to Shibuya. But let us not dwell on why this image is used. For us, studying Japan, we can acknowledge that it reflects a reality of what Japan is like today. For us, what is of significance is to study what is inside the image itself and how that reflects aspects of Japanese society and culture.

TŌKYŌ – THE MEGACITY

Tōkyō is Japan's capital and its biggest city. I expect that you managed to identify it as one of Japan's biggest cities as part of Exercise 1.4. But do you know how big its population is? And how does it compare to other major cities around the world? It is not uncommon to come across television programmes and websites that claim that Tōkyō is the most populated city in the world with a population of over 30 million. However, such a figure is very misleading as it is not the population of Tōkyō alone, but includes the cities that border it, not only within Tōkyō prefecture, but also neighbouring prefectures. While it is undoubtedly the case that it is hard to notice the boundaries between Tōkyō, Kawasaki and Yokohama, for example, they are three separate cities. In fact, the population of the 23 wards of Tōkyō is about 9 million (Tōkyō Metropolitan Government 2014), and so is barely half-a-million more than New York (New York City 2014) or London (Greater London Authority 2014). But while the population of these three cities may be comparable, the layout of them varies significantly.

For a visitor to New York, most of the main sights are contained with Manhattan. Even from the northern end of Central Park to Brooklyn Bridge is 11 km. The centre of London is even smaller, and although many people's understanding of the location of places is based on the underground map, this map is not a geographical representation of where things are, and in reality it is possible to walk between most points within the area covered by the Circle Line. From Notting Hill at the western side of the Circle Line to Liverpool Street on the eastern side is 8 km. Within the Circle Line of London or within Manhattan in New York are the hearts of the two cities. But Tōkyō is different; its centre is 'empty', as Barthes (1983: 30) described it. Barthes' view of the city was perhaps influenced by historical maps of the city, where the Imperial Palace often appears at the centre and due to the hidden nature of the Palace and what goes on there probably added to Barthes' feeling of emptiness. For most today, their geographical understanding of Tōkyō is based upon the 'circular' Yamanote Line.

The Yamanote Line is 34.5 km long and the distance between its northern and southern extremes is about 13 km, while the distance between its western and eastern extremes is about 6 km. So the circular nature is more in terms of the train services themselves than the shape of the route (see Figure 2.2), although it is not uncommon for the diagram to be simplified to a more circular or elliptical shape. But while it is certainly an exaggeration to suggest that the centre of the Yamanote Line is empty, the significance of the line is that it connects the many hearts of Tōkyō. For Tōkyō does not have a single place from where the life of the city radiates, but multiple 'centres' – such as Ueno, Ikebukuro, Shinjuku and Shibuya. From many of these 'centres', further railway lines radiate out into the suburbs and off to other cities, meaning that the stations become important hubs for interchange. But they are destinations in their own right too, each with their distinctive atmosphere and offerings, such as the financial district of Marunouchi, which lies between Tōkyō station on the eastern side of the loop and the Imperial Palace only 1 km to its west. Shibuya is one of these 'centres' into which people from not only Tōkyō, but other cities pour.

While the population of Tōkyō is often exaggerated, one aspect of its size that cannot be ignored is the population density. At 6,029 people per km^2 (Tōkyō Metropolitan Government 2013). But it is important to remember that Tōkyō is not Japan and Japan is not Tōkyō. Later on, we will discuss the issues of depopulation across the country and how not all of Japan is so crowded. Tōkyō is crowded and densely populated, and with people from other cities coming into the city at times too it is hardly a surprise that it is possible to find an image of Tōkyō having crowded streets. Such an image is an accurate reflection of one aspect of life in Tōkyō. The Shibuya scramble crossing performs this role well.

Let us return to Figure 2.1 again. Towering over the people below are the buildings covered with neon signs and large screens. Compared to the skyscrapers of many modern cities, the buildings around Shibuya are relatively short. Of course, there are skyscrapers in Tōkyō; most are located around the Yamanote Line 'centres' of Shinjuku, Ikebukuro, Marunouchi (near Tōkyō station) and Shiodome (near Shimbashi station), as well as Roppongi within the Yamanote Line itself. An aerial view of Tōkyō consequently reveals the somewhat disparate nature of the

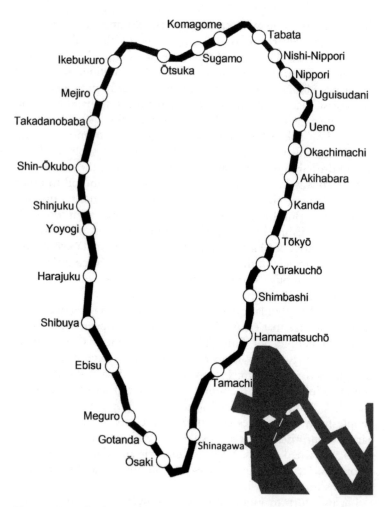

Figure 2.2 Map of Tōkyō's centres

city when compared to many cities where the skyscrapers are concentrated around where the financial hub of the city is. But while the height of the buildings in Shibuya may be unremarkable, their facades are impressive. What do these screens and signs tell us about Japan?

One of the screens is often broadcasting the news. For a country that is considered to be news hungry and have such a high television viewing figures, perhaps this should be of no surprise. Another way in which Japanese people's thirst for news is supposedly seen is that Japan has the highest number of newspapers sold on a daily basis (Nikkei 2014). However, it is important to stress that high readership and high purchase are not the same thing. What Japan undeniably has is the latter. What is less certain is how much the newspapers are being read. While I was living in Japan, I was subjected to some very hard sales techniques – including suggestions that the salesman would not get a bonus and be able to feed his family if I did not take out a newspaper subscription. Why would such techniques be used? Approximately 95 per cent of all newspaper sales are by subscription (Nikkei 2014). Many households have more than one subscription – for example, having the *Nikkei Shimbun* for business news, a sports newspaper for sports and tabloid-like news, and one of the major national newspapers for general news stories. They may also subscribe to a local newspaper. Many papers have both morning and evening editions, although sales for the latter are significantly lower (Hood 2011: 148). But while each of the papers has the potential to serve a different purpose due to their specialisms, it may not be that they are used for these reasons at all. For example, I have seen some families use a paper merely to check the television listings – this hardly equates to newspaper readership.

In a similar vein, we need to be cautious about the figures regarding television consumption. Heinze (2011) points out that while the TV may be on for about eight hours per day, it may not always be the key activity. Indeed, in Japan I have often seen situations where the television is seemingly there to provide background noise rather than being the focal point of the individual or family's activities. Japan has a number of TV channels, which can be separated into three main categories: those provided by NHK, which is funded by a TV license fee, commercial national networks and commercial local TV channels. The fact that NHK is funded by a license fee may lead some to assume that it is similar to the BBC in the UK, but NHK does not show the range of entertainment programmes that may be found on the BBC. NHK has also experienced significant political interference (Krauss 2000). For commercial channels, it is the influence of advertisers that is apparent. Programmes themselves may be sponsored by a number of companies and include product placements in some form, as well as there being commercial breaks during the transmission. The issue we need to keep in mind is the degree to which TV channels may adjust their content to appease advertisers.

Advertising also features heavily in the scene in Shibuya. Indeed, advertising is seemingly everywhere in Japan. It can appear on the sides of planes and trains, on flyers inside trains and on telephone poles, on signs outside buildings, inside magazines and newspapers, and on commercial television. The total advertising expenditure in Japan in 2012 was estimated to be about ¥5,900 billion, which represents 1.24 per cent of Japan's gross domestic product (GDP) (Dentsū 2013: 20). To put that figure into perspective, it is more than the Japanese government spends on defence, public works or education (Ministry of Finance 2013: 5). Whether any of this advertising is effective is beyond the scope of what we are focusing on here, but we need to be aware of its scale and how we can use it as a tool to study aspects of Japanese society. Changes in what is advertised, where the advertisements are and how they appear (for example, print media, signs or moving images) will be a reflection of variations in Japanese society.

One of the changes over the twentieth century in the way advertisements are presented was naturally the adoption of bright electronic signs, which over time have also become like TV screens showing moving images. Such signs require electricity. How can such developments happen in a country that often claims to have little in the way of natural resources? While Japan does have some limited coal resources, for example, 84 per cent of its energy requirements are imported (World Nuclear Association 2014), and this has significant consequences for how it conducts its international relations with certain countries. For other energy needs, Japan turned to nuclear power. This is perhaps surprising given the country's experience at the hands of atomic weapons in 1945, but by 2010 it accounted for nearly one-third of all electricity production (World Nuclear Association 2014). This rise was not merely a reflection of a national policy, but also the dynamics of local politics, as we will discuss in the next chapter. Nuclear power was seemingly accepted by most Japanese people. However, all that changed on 11 March 2011. Although the events of that day will be discussed in more detail in Chapter 8, what is pertinent here is that the problems at the Fukushima Dai-ichi Nuclear Power Plant led many Japanese people to question the country's use of nuclear power. The nuclear power stations were all turned off, meaning the country became heavily reliant upon importing oil and gas again, while renewable energy also began to be more heavily promoted, as we will discuss further in Chapter 4.

THE COST OF LIVING

Let us take another look at Figure 2.1 and now think about the people in the picture. Who are they and where are they going? The answer for many relates to the fact that Shibuya is a major shopping and entertainment centre in Tōkyō. Before we consider what people may be spending their money on, let us first think about one of the problems that Japan appeared to be grappling with for many years – people not spending money.

You are probably familiar with the concept of inflation and that it is often seen as being a problem. The logic for this is simple – if there is inflation of prices (i.e. prices are increasing), then people will need to spend a larger proportion of their income if they continue to purchase the same items. Alternatively, they will need to change their spending habits or seek a means to increase their income. But in Japan, the issue for many years in the 1990s and early twenty-first century has not been inflation, but deflation. Why is deflation such a problem? To put it simply, if there is deflation, why should people buy something today when they know that by waiting, it is likely that the price will fall and so they will be able to save some of their money? If people wait before consuming, then consumer spending will fall and the parts of the economy that rely upon sales will be impacted. Companies need to find ways to encourage people to spend money; this could be through further reductions or special offers or through trying to stimulate a feeling of a need to consume now by advertising, for example. The government may also try to develop schemes to try to encourage spending, as we have seen in Japan. Of course, we must not forget that the issue of deflation applies not only to individual consumers, but also to company spending.

When it comes to looking at what Japanese people spend their money on, it is perhaps worth putting it into context by showing some international comparisons. However, doing this poses problems. The first of these is that people in different countries do not buy the same things. This behaviour is a reflection of variations in cultures. So whereas rice is an important part of the diet in Japan, for example, it is not so significant in the UK, where potatoes tend to be consumed more. Including potatoes in the basket, therefore, would not truly reflect what Japanese are spending their money on. If the product, such as rice, is not produced in one country and it has to import it, then this is also likely to distort the price in comparison to a country that does produce rice. To get around these problems, we can do a comparison grouping areas of spending together (see Table 2.1) to show the relative differences in spending on food as a whole compared with spending on education, for example. Another problem with doing such an international comparison revolves around the issue of exchange rates. To better understand the impact that exchange rates have, please complete Exercise 2.1 (p. 34).

If we think back to Exercise 1.1, perhaps among the items that you listed as being symbolic of Japan were aspects of its food culture, and we have seen in Table 2.1 that food accounts for a large proportion of spending. In 2013, Japan's cuisine was added to UNESCO's 'Intangible Cultural Heritage List' (UNESCO 2014). While it is natural that the contents of many meals that Japanese eat may be different to other countries, there are also variations in the overall experience too. Most Japanese restaurants will contain either wax models of the food they serve in the front window or will have photographs of the food on the menu. For those visiting the country without any knowledge of the language, this has the advantage that you can point to the desired item. But the overwhelming majority of customers will be Japanese, so what is the benefit to them of this visual presentation of the menu and what does it tell us about Japan? As you consider the answer to these questions, some points to think about are the inclusive

Table 2.1 Share of expenditure in Japan, USA, UK and Canada (2009)

Category	Japan	USA	UK	Canada
Food				
Food at home	17.2	13.6	8.6	11.6
Food away from home	4.6	6.3	6.0	3.7
Food total	21.8	19.9	14.6	15.3
Housing	21.6	26.3	24.1	21.4
Transportation				
Automobiles	2.2	5.1	6.1	8.3
Public transportation	2.3	2.5	1.1	2.0
All other transportation	5.3	7.6	10.3	10.2
Transportation total	9.8	15.2	17.5	20.6
Health care	4.3	7.2	1.4	4.2
Clothing	4.2	4.0	5.5	6.0
Education	4.0	2.4	1.8	2.6
Culture/entertainment/ recreation	11.2	6.5	15.1	8.6
Alcoholic beverages and tobacco products	1.6	1.9	4.8	3.2
Other categories	21.6	19.6	12.2	18.1

Note: Other categories include miscellaneous categories that are unique to a particular country so that direct comparison is not possible.

Source: Table by the author based on Table 1 of Bureau of Labor Statistics (2012).

nature of such a system since even children – who may not be able to read the *kanji* on written menus – can be a part of the selection process, that perhaps most Japanese respond strongly to visual input and that the system of using wax models has ensured the development of other businesses.

Another difference in the eating out culture can be observed at the end of the meal, for in Japan tips are not given. In the USA, tips of 20 per cent are often expected, whereas in the UK tips are typically 10 per cent. Clearly, this represents a relative

EXERCISE 2.1

Let us assume that a car in Japan costs ¥3,000,000. What would the price be elsewhere? Complete the first table to see what the impact is on the price of a new car when using exchange rates from a number of different dates. If the currency your country uses is not listed, you should look these up too. In the second table, calculate what the price of oil would be in yen for these dates, using the average dollar price for a barrel of oil for that year.

Car price: ¥3,000,000

Date	$		£		ff (ECU until 1999)	
	Rate	Price	Rate	Price	Rate	Price
January 1985	253.76		286.92		173.51	
January 1990	144.94		239.03		174.31	
January 1995	99.73		156.98		125.44	
January 2000	105.10		172.30		106.53	
January 2005	103.36		194.10		135.62	
January 2010	91.32		147.59		130.34	

Price of crude oil

Date	1985	1990	1995	2000	2005	2010
Price of one barrel ($)	27.56	23.73	17.02	28.50	54.52	79.50
Exchange rate	253.76	144.94	99.73	105.10	103.36	91.32
Price of one barrel (¥)						

Source: Exchange rates taken from FX Top (2014). Price of oil taken from BP (2014).

saving to those in Japan, but what does the lack of tips tell us? Tips in other countries are typically there to allow the customer to reward good service, although often the tips are seemingly expected regardless of the quality of service and food, and they are a means to boost the often relatively low pay that the staff receive. However, in Japan variations in the level of service provided would be unusual. Training staff to provide a professional service is a key part of many businesses, as we will be discussing further in Chapter 5. That all staff should provide an expected level of service may be one reason why performance-related pay has not been widely adopted in Japan, although there has been a move in this direction in the past decade or so (Olcott 2009: 146). But all this does not mean that those in Japan cannot reward a good experience or punish a poor experience. To show that they liked the restaurant and service, they will return to the same place or recommend it to a friend. Repeat business and personal recommendations are often much more effective in establishing a good business model than seeking out new custom. Travellers may not be in a position to punish or reward in the same way due to the brevity of their visit, but the impact upon them of such a system can be seen in the large number of travel guides that include reviews of individual restaurants.

Although many cities have seen the rise of large supermarkets in recent years, a ubiquitous feature of the shopping experience in Japan is the convenience store. These stores offer a range of goods and services including food, drink, household goods, books, magazines, clothing, stationery and a collection point for courier services. Many convenience stores are also open 24 hours a day. Is there really a need for such shops to be open throughout the night? While these are businesses, so one would assume that they will only operate in conditions that return a profit, the overall model for the business is that they are available when the customer needs them, not when the shop dictates, and so it may be that staying open becomes a defence mechanism as the company cannot get a reputation as one that is not always convenient. But convenience is not limited to shops, as machines selling drinks and snacks or other goods are seen along seemingly every road in Japan. While this may reflect a Japanese desire for convenience, that such machines can exist, sometimes in somewhat isolated locations, is also a reflection of the relative lack of crime in Japan, as we will discuss further in Chapter 7.

While this section has concentrated on the cost of living and consumption, it is worth briefly mentioning the issue of savings in Japan. In 2012, workers' households had savings of ¥12.33 million, which is 78.4 per cent higher than the yearly income (Ministry of Internal Affairs and Communications 2013: 149). We will discuss one of the implications of this in Chapter 8.

WOMEN ARE KEY

When we think about consumer spending in Japan, we need to not only think about what is being bought, but also who is doing the spending. In this respect, arguably the most important group are women. Females make up 51.4 per cent of the population (Ministry of Internal Affairs and Communications 2013: 12) and they tend to be key consumers as they delay marriage and have high levels of disposable income (JMRN 2007: 3). In family households, it is still not uncommon for the women to take care of the household finances, with them effectively giving their husband, who is likely to be the main salary earner, pocket money. Consequently, we would expect to see the importance of the female market to be reflected in not only the products that are developed, but how they are marketed. This may not even be restricted to physical products sold in shops, but may be seen in relation to films and productions for TV and other forms of entertainment (see Chapter 7).

Although men are often still the main salary earner in a family, Japan has seen an increase in the number of dual-income households where the wife is also earning money (Fujiwara 2008). However, we need to think about whether the types of work and their reward are comparable, and if not why not, and what this reflects and what its possible impact may be. Female participation rate in labour force is 48.2 per cent, compared to 70.8 per cent for males (Ministry of Internal Affairs and Communications 2013: 127), and women predominantly account for non-regular staff (see below). Overall, the position for women does not seem that positive. Indeed, this is a point that was made in a *New York Times* article (23 August 2013). However, while this article effectively 'put Japan in the backwoods' (Kinmonth, personal communication) in comparison to the USA, it overlooked how even the USA is below the OECD average and that there are parts of the USA where the figure is considerably worse than in much of Japan (Kinmonth, personal communication).

With many readers' relative lack of knowledge and connection to Japan, it is seemingly easy for foreign journalists to use Japanese examples as a means to help foster a belief in the superiority of their own country, painting over the serious issues that may exist in their own country, by cherry-picking the figures that suit.

Despite the guarantees for equality set out in the Constitution and the 1985 Equal Opportunities Law and the subsequent revisions to it, clearly equality is missing. Many women do not get the same full contract employee status (*seishain*) as their male counterparts when entering large companies, and so women account for most non-regular staff (Ministry of Internal Affairs and Communications 2013: 134). It appears that there is still an expectation among many Japanese companies for women to leave the company when they become pregnant with their first child (*The Japan Times*, 23 September 2013). When women look to return to employment, it is most likely that they will be employed in relatively unskilled part-time jobs. It is no wonder, then, that we see so few female managers in large Japanese companies; less than 10 per cent at section chief or above at 81 per cent of companies (*The Japan Times*, 15 August 2013). It is not only companies where we see few women in high-profile positions. In the National Diet in 2013, there only 7.9 per cent of politicians were female (UN Data 2014) and there were only two women in the 19-person Cabinet, suggesting the target of having 30 per cent of senior government positions being held by women by 2020 (Japan Today, 26 September 2013) may be hard to achieve. Although perhaps not a view that is widely held, Yōichi Masazoe, who was elected governor of Tōkyō in 2014, had previously suggested that women were not suited to being politicians due to their menstrual cycle making them 'abnormal' (Fukushima 2014). It was clearly a reflection of the challenge that some women face in trying to get equality.

That women drop out from employment when starting a new family is not restricted solely to Japan. When mapped on to a graph showing employment rates against age, it leads to what is referred to as an 'M-curve' due to the dip in the middle of the curve when compared to men. The size of the dip has undoubtedly reduced in Japan in recent decades, but the questions to ask are what can be done to reduce the dip further and are the jobs that women are returning to if they have left employment to have a family appropriate. Of course, we should not overlook the fact that many women do want to become a housewife (Japan Today, 26 September 2013) and part-time work can provide the flexibility in hours that they may be looking for, although we need to keep in mind that such work also does not provide the types of benefits found with regular work. As pointed out, one poll by the Ministry of Health, Labour and Welfare found that about one-third of women in Japan want to be a housewife and not work once married, and this was the headline of articles that featured the story. However, the figure was still 4 per cent lower than the number that do want to work. But we can see that being a house-wife in Japan may still be regarded with higher status than the equivalent in some Western societies. One should not overlook the fact that the expectations, both of the women themselves as well as society, have been, and sometimes continue to be, different to that in some other societies (Condon 1991: 295). You also need to be thinking about these issues within the context of some of the other challenges that Japan is facing.

Japan is facing a demographic challenge. I do not want to call it a problem, for that immediately casts it in a negative light and we should aim to avoid such a subjective position from the start. Since the early 1970s, the total fertility rate, that is the number of children a woman will have in her lifetime, for women in Japan has been below 2.1, the typical level required to maintain the population at its current level. Think about 10 of your married relations and friends that you know and the number of children they have. For a rate of 2.1 to be met, nine of the people you have selected need to have had two children and the other to have had three (or some similar combination to get to a total of 21 children). Do not be surprised if you find the total figure to be below 21 – many countries are facing the challenges that Japan are. While the media may focus on the population of the planet as a whole growing, the long-term trend in many countries is to follow what has happened in Japan. As you read this book and study Japan, you may want to think about the challenges that Japan has faced, how it has faced them and what lessons could be learnt for your own country, keeping in mind that there may be many reasons why your country may be able to, or want to, do things differently.

The Japanese population is now in decline. Having peaked at just over 128 million in 2010, in 2012 it fell by over a quarter of a million (Ministry of Internal Affairs and Communications, 2013: 12). That is the equivalent of a whole city being wiped off the map. Of course, in reality the population is not being wiped off from one location, but across much of the country, as we will discuss in Chapter 3. By 2050, the population is expected to fall below 100 million. The impact of Japan's changing demographics is that it is estimated that Japan has a skilled labour shortage. One way to address this is to introduce further automation for unskilled jobs and to train people to become more skilled to plug the gap in skilled labour shortage. Another alternative is to allow mass immigration of skilled labour from other countries. As we will discuss in Chapter 6, this is probably not a realistic option on a large scale, although we have certainly seen shifts, and this is why we are seeing graduates in Japanese studies from universities around the world become increasingly in demand. A third alternative is to have more women remain or join the skilled labour force. Assuming that there are women that wish to do this, we need to think about what some of the challenges may be in achieving this. As you continue to read this book, keep issues such as this in mind.

But addressing the skilled labour shortage is not the only demand that is being placed on women. The Japanese government would also like to see them having more babies. Not only that, but it would like them to have babies sooner. Of course, if this were to happen it would be a longer-term solution to the issues the government is seeking to address since the children will not enter the workplace for many years (and until then, they are a further drain on the government's funding due to the provision of education). Furthermore, it could also see women being out of the workforce for longer, which runs counter to the other demands being put on them. The reality is, though, as we have discussed, many women in Japan only have one child. What are the reasons for this? The answer, or answers, to this are likely to vary. Economic reasons – for example, the cost of education and general costs – may be one of them, although the amount of savings that many Japanese have would suggest that this may not be by any means the main reason for all. So what other things do we need to consider? What about the working practices at companies that mean that men, in particular, will work long hours or go out drinking? It seems probable that the less time a man is at home, the less chance there is any interaction with his partner and so the chances of having a child are further reduced. Does the fact that many live away from their older relatives (see Chapter 3) mean that a lack of childcare provision is putting off some from having children?

Japan has seen a trend seen in many developed nations, in that the average age at which women first get married has been rising. Whereas when it came to finding a bride Japanese women were said to be like Christmas cakes – up to 25 (cf. 25 December), they were highly desirable but after that they were no longer wanted – we now see that the average age at which Japanese women are getting married was 29.2 years old in 2012 compared to 23.0 in 1950. Similarly, the average for men has risen to 30.8 from 25.9 (Ministry of Internal Affairs and Communications 2013: 21). The age at which a woman has her first child has also been rising, although we also need to keep in mind the changing nature of firstborn children in Japan. Whereas a large proportion of babies used to be 'honeymoon babies', born within the first year of marriage, now about a quarter of children are *dekichatta-ko*, where the mother has become pregnant prior to marriage (Tokuhiro 2009: 16). This often leads to shotgun weddings so as to avoid the reduced inheritance illegitimate children are entitled to, although this law was ruled to be unconstitutional in 2013 (Senda 2013). Avoiding having children outside of wedlock is reflected in the fact that only around 2 per cent of babies are born to unmarried women in Japan (cf. 50 per cent in France and 40 per cent in the USA) (Senda 2013). On top of this, there are approximately 250,000 abortions or 9.3 per 1,000 women, which is much lower than in many other industrialised nations (*The Japan Times*, 20 October 2009). The rate has dropped significantly since the 1950s, although it is thought that official figures are likely to be lower than the true figure due to some not being reported. However, the large number of *dekichatta-ko* may also suggest that there are now a relatively large proportion of marriages where the couple had a relationship before marriage rather than the marriage being an arranged marriage. The degree to which this will change the nature of families in Japan, the impact it will have on happiness and on the divorce rate is something you may wish to consider further.

While the number of babies being born may have reduced over the post-war period and the Japanese population is in decline, the picture is by no means uniform across the country. Indeed, what we appear to be seeing is that the cities are continuing to grow, while smaller towns and villages are in terminal decline. This is an issue that we will return to in Chapter 3 when we think about some of the other factors – beyond the convenience and jobs that larger cities tend to offer – that have led to this situation developing. Let us again consider the total fertility rate. Table 2.2 shows the 20 countries with the lowest rates (see overleaf). Look also at Table 2.3 (p. 43), which shows the 10 prefectures in Japan with the highest rates (many of which have seen their rates increase in the past few years) and the 10 prefectures with the lowest rates (some of which have also seen increased in recent years). While nowhere in Japan has a rate above 2.1, we can see that many prefectures are higher than countries with the lower rates, and Japan itself is comparable to many other countries. The question that you need to be asking is what are the reasons for the regional differences since clearly the lack of uniformity across Japan shows that there cannot be anything common to all Japanese. This is yet another example of why we have to be very careful when making generalisations about Japan or relying too heavily on average figures.

HOUSING

One of the key determinates of price is the interaction of supply and demand. If supply remains the same but demand increases, then price would be expected to rise. Consequently, in large cities where the room to build remains largely constant, as more people want to live there, so the price of land will be expected to increase. This can be further exaggerated by the problems of supplying the construction materials. Although the development of skyscrapers and apartment blocks is a means to increase the available living and workspace of a city, so could help to arrest some of the increase, the impact is seemingly negligible.

Table 2.2 OECD countries with the lowest fertility rates (2008)

	Country	Rate
20=	China	1.77
	Netherlands	1.77
22	Canada	1.68
23	Estonia	1.66
24	Luxembourg	1.60
25	Slovenia	1.53
26	Greece	1.51
27	Czech Republic	1.50
28	Russian Federation	1.49
29	Switzerland	1.48
30	Spain	1.46
31	Italy	1.42
32	Austria	1.41
33	Poland	1.39
34	Germany	1.38
35=	Japan	1.37
	Portugal	1.37
37	Hungary	1.35
38	Slovak Republic	1.32
39	Korea	1.19
	OECD Average	1.75

Source: OECD (2014).

In the 1980s, the price of land in Japan skyrocketed. Naturally, this was centred on Tōkyō, although increases were seen across the country, and particularly in the larger cities. At one point, it was said that the value of the land of the Imperial Palace was the same as the whole of California. Think about that. How could it be that such a small area could be worth the same as all the economic activity in cities such as San Francisco and Los Angeles? You could not even fit the studios of Hollywood into the Imperial Palace, let alone the high-tech companies based in Silicon Valley. One day, this reality hit home and the price of land crashed, leading to financial problems for many individuals and companies

Table 2.3 Prefectures with the highest and lowest fertility rates (2009)

	Prefectures with highest rates	Rate
1	Okinawa	1.79
2	Miyazaki	1.61
3	Kumamoto	1.58
4	Kagoshima	1.56
5=	Fukui	1.55
	Shimane	1.55
7=	Nagasaki	1.50
	Ōita	1.50
9=	Fukushima	1.49
	Saga	1.49
	Prefectures with lowest rates	Rate
38	Kōchi	1.29
39=	Saitama	1.28
	Kanagawa	1.28
	Ōsaka	1.28
42	Aomori	1.26
43	Miyagi	1.25
44	Nara	1.23
45	Kyōto	1.20
46	Hokkaidō	1.19
47	Tōkyō	1.12

Source: Ministry of Health, Labour and Welfare (2014).

since they had finances (loans and rents, for example) based on the higher price.

In Chapter 3, we will discuss the price of land further and the disparities across Japan, but here let us consider the way in which price impacts housing. As the price of land increases, so the price of housing (i.e. purchasing a house or rental costs) can be expected to increase. One should not be surprised, therefore, to find a demand for smaller plots of land when the price of land is high. In other words, some may prefer to live in a small flat compared to a house. Also, for those looking to purchase a house, a garden may be seen as a luxury that cannot be afforded. On the other side of the equation, those who own land may look to sell their garden to a developer so that they can get additional income. The consequence of this can be seen in Japanese cities where buildings are tightly packed together. However, we need to be careful not to oversimplify this to an economic argument. If we look at homes in the countryside where land is more affordable and where the land may be in the family for many generations, we also rarely see homes with large gardens. You should consider what the reasons may be for this as you continue your studies of Japan and also what the implications of it may be.

Putting aside that many Japanese may actually wish to live in smaller accommodation, we should also be careful not to over-exaggerate the apparent differences in housing between Japan and many other developed nations. An infamous EC Commission internal memo in the 1970s described Japanese housing as being like rabbit hutches. The travel writer Michael Palin put it even more bluntly when he suggested that:

All these towns seem to be alike, and considering how important a part aesthetics play in Japanese culture, remarkably unattractive. There is a constant feeling of being cramped. The houses are small and narrow, the streets have no pavements, the architecture of a shanty town in Ethiopia is more inventive.

(Palin 1997: 53–5)

But what is the point of making the outside of a building attractive if there are limited opportunities to see it? If the buildings are close together and there is no garden in which to sit and see the house, one has to assume that the motivation to maintain the exterior appearance would be missing. When improvements are done, it is more likely that an interior room will be remodelled than the exterior. We also need to be careful to compare like with like. While many in Palin's native UK may have houses with gardens, in larger cities this is not possible. I have come across many Japanese who have been as appalled by the sight of Britain's terraced housing as Palin seemingly is by Japan's cramped, but always detached, housing.

But what about the interior of these Japanese houses and flats? If we consider the amount of living space rather than include the footprint of the house and any garden, then Japan may not seem so bad. However, space will often be at a premium and so there is limited room for storage. While many houses will have a traditional Japanese room with *tatami* flooring, which may be kept relatively free of clutter, many other rooms will often be seem very distant from the minimalistic style idealised by many non-Japanese designers that claim to have been influenced by a Japanese style of living. The relative lack of space in the home can have a wide range of impacts (see Figure 2.3). It can also lead to many Japanese doing

Figure 2.3 Space pressures. Top left: the lack of space in homes has led to the development of cat cafés where people can go to play with cats. Top right: the lack of space in the city leads to some very small parks being squeezed between buildings. Bottom left: the lack of space and thinness of walls has been amongst the factors contributing to the development of 'love hotels', such as these in Shibuya, where rooms can be rented by the hour as well as for over-night stays. Bottom middle: a multi-purpose room that can be used for socialising as well as a bedroom, while outside a very narrow garden separates the house from the wall of the neighbour's house. Bottom right: the lack of space and opportunity to access nature elsewhere has led to the development of a fishing pond in central Tōkyō.

regular small shops rather than a weekly large shop. In big cities, the problems of accessing shops by car also means that shopping is likely to be done on foot, possibly in combination with using public transport, or by bike. Both of these limit how much can be bought, and so you should think about the impact on what is likely to be bought when people use particular types of shops and even what impact it has on where shops will be located.

SUMMARY

In this chapter, we have looked at some of the demographic challenges that Japan faces and how these get played out in the big cities such as Tōkyō. From starting with the familiar image of the scramble crossing in Shibuya, one of Tōkyō's many centres, we have discussed the importance of consumer spending and how women are central to this, but also to a wide range of issues that Japan is facing. The chapter finished by considering the impact of the country's limited space and demographic pressures on housing. Throughout the chapter, we have seen how it is important not to assume that Japanese have the same expectations as we may have and that we need to be careful how to use general statistics when significant regional differences may exist. This is an issue that will be highlighted further in the next chapter when we consider the impact that intercity transportation has had on Japan.

3

JAPAN ON THE MOVE

Japan is busy. As we discussed in Chapter 2, Japan has some large cities and houses are close together due to lack of gardens, and has many apartment buildings. One impact of this is that there will be more people within walking distance of a single point than one may find in comparable sized cities in many other nations. Consequently, Japan lends itself to rail travel. The image of people being literally pushed on to trains by station employees is heavily used by the media. But this image is not as used as another that relates to Japanese railways: a *shinkansen* ('bullet train') passing Mount Fuji (see Figure 3.1), which you may have even included within your answers to Exercise 1.1.

This chapter will discuss what can be learnt about Japan from its transportation system. First, we will look at the development of the *shinkansen*, including why it is so safe and how it runs on time, and what these aspects tell us about Japan. We will also look at what the varieties of trains themselves tell us about the operating companies and the areas they serve. But Japan does not only have a high-speed railway network; there are also a plethora of airports across the country. How can this be? What does this tell us about the way that politics and business operate in Japan? The chapter will then look at what the impact is on Japan of its intercity transportation system and how not everything may be as positive as it was expected to be.

Figure 3.1 A *shinkansen* passing Mount Fuji

WELCOME TO THE *SHINKANSEN*

1 October 1964 was a momentous day. It marked the start of a transport revolution not only for Japan, but for the world as a whole. Just as many countries were embracing cars and heralding the age of jet planes, Japan demonstrated the relevance of railways. While Japan was perhaps not on the radar for the world news ordinarily, in October 1964 the world's media was in Japan for the Tōkyō Olympics. With some events being held in Ōsaka, a trip on the *shinkansen* became a necessity and so articles about Japan's technological prowess were inevitable.

The Tōkaidō Shinkansen was an instant success, and soon proposals for a *shinkansen* network criss-crossing Japan were put forward. Although these plans had to be scaled back due to the economic challenges of the early 1970s, the network today covers much of Japan. But the expanding network came at a price. During the 1970s, the finances of Japanese National Railways (JNR) worsened due to a combination of the construction costs of the *shinkansen* and due to management issues (Kasai 2003: 39). In the 1980s, the prime minister, Yasuhiro Nakasone, made reforming JNR one of his top goals. As well as trying to find a solution to the financial problems, he took aim at the management of JNR and the influence of the unions (Hood 2006a: 107). The result was that in 1987, JNR was broken up into six regionally based passenger companies, with Honshū split into three and one each in Hokkaidō, Kyūshū and Shikoku, as well as one nation-wide freight company. The regional split was not totally neat; for example, in relation to the *shinkansen* there are areas where lines effectively run through territories of other companies. It is import-ant to be aware that the seven JR companies, as the former JNR companies are collectively known, are not Japan's only railway companies. Indeed, there are over 200 companies. Many of these are providing passenger services over relatively short distances, in many cases competing with other private companies or JR companies, and a large proportion of these companies' incomes often comes from activities other than the railways such as shops at stations. Indeed, in Japan stations are not seen as places merely to go to catch a train, but will often include shops, theatres and other facilities. Increasingly, the designs have been improved with those on newer *shinkansen* lines, including features that reflect the local city in some way, and this can help, at least initially, with a renewed identity and reinvigoration of the local economy (as we will discuss below). Although the railway com-panies are competitors, there are also times where companies collaborate, as can be seen with the through running of some overground trains on the underground network in Tōkyō.

Let us now consider some of the key features of the *shinkansen*. The average delay on the Tōkaidō Shinkansen, for example, is 30 seconds (JR Tōkai 2013: 6). How can this be achieved? Time is crucial. Anything over one minute is officially classified as being late. This compares to 10 minutes in the UK, 14 minutes in France and 15 minutes in Italy, for example (Mito 2002: 7). Training at the companies is strict and drivers learn to respect the clock. Indeed, employees will receive a pocket watch upon starting at the company, and there is even a space for this clock alongside the high-tech monitors on the dashboard of trains (see Figure 5.4). Training centres have a range of facilities and computers for employees to practise and be tested on. Through the training, the staff are taught to physically acknowledge signals by pointing and making verbal comments. Drivers are expected to stop the *shinkansen*, which may be around 400m long, within 15cm of a particular point on the platform. Stopping at the correct point is critical, as there will also be markings for where passengers should be lining up. In other words, being punctual also requires the cooperation of the passengers. The result is that trains will often only stop at stations for 50 seconds.

Safety is at the heart of the *shinkansen*. There are special trains that run at normal *shinkansen* operating speeds but go along testing for defects in the line and electrical cables, for example, using lasers and such like. These trains are used on a regular basis and will also come out after a significant earthquake to check the infrastructure. *Shinkansen* lines are closed from midnight to 06:00 every day for any maintenance work to be done. This is a different system to that seen in many countries, when maintenance will sometimes see closure of lines or speed restrictions put in place on Sundays or during school holidays. To further help maintain safety, there is also a system known as Automatic Train Control (ATC). ATC keeps track of what the safe maximum speed of the train is, taking into account where the next train is on the line and whether there is a corner coming up, for example. Should the driver be going too fast, the breaks will automatically be applied. An important point to keep in mind is that the driver is in control; the ATC is there to support the driver. Thanks to the training and ATC, there have been no collisions between *shinkansen* during its history. It also has helped lead to the concept that you can set your watch by the *shinkansen*. However, we must keep in mind the possible negative aspects of the focus on time. Although not a *shinkansen* service, but a conventional line service, Japan's worst rail crash in recent years occurred when a train derailed as the driver tried to make up some lost time. The result was that 107 were killed in the accident on 25 April 2005. The cause was seen, at least by much of the Japanese media at the time, to be in part as a result of the pressure on drivers to adhere to the schedule.

Two of the *shinkansen* lines, the Akita Shinkansen and Yamagata Shinkansen, are commonly referred to as 'mini-*shinkansen*' rather than full specification *shinkansen*. The difference stems from the fact that the gauge of Japanese railways is typically narrower than the 'standard' gauge found in many countries. The *shinkansen* is standard gauge. However, on both the Japanese narrow gauge and on the *shinkansen* train carriages tend to be wider than would be found elsewhere, allowing the trains to carry more people. But when it comes to the mini-*shinkansen* lines, as the tunnels were designed for trains on a narrower gauge, the carriage has to be narrower than standard *shinkansen* carriages. This is not the only difference. More significantly, there are also level crossings, which are not found on main *shinkansen* lines. Accidents at level crossings account for about 50 per cent of all railway accidents in Japan (Hood 2006a: 133), although I think designating them solely as railway accidents rather than road or pedestrian accidents is not necessarily appropriate. As the mini-*shinkansen* lines have level crossings, the top speeds on these lines are lower than the main *shinkansen* lines. So why do these two lines exist? The fundamental answer is that it speeds up the overall journey for those going to, say, Tōkyō. As there is no need to change trains at the main *shinkansen* station, a saving of at least 10 minutes can be made. Although such a saving may not sound like much, in the battle with planes to have the quickest door-to-door travel time, each minute can count. In reality, the time saving is greater than this, as although the trains cannot operate at the same speeds as they do on the main *shinkansen* lines, the improvement in infrastructure will still allow for an increase in speeds over conventional rail services. Another advantage that mini-*shinkansen* have is that it is relatively cheap to upgrade a line to this specification when compared to building a full specification *shinkansen*. It is unlikely that without using this system Akita and Yamagata would ever have been served by any form of *shinkansen*. We will discuss the battle between the *shinkansen* and planes further below.

The *shinkansen* lines are not all the same. The size and number of the cities they serve varies, for example. As a result, the trains have come to reflect these differences, as well as differences in the focus of their operating companies. While to the casual observer many of the differences may not be obvious, in trying to understand how Japan operates and being mindful of differences that may exist across the country, you need to be looking out for subtle variations and then try to find explanations for what is causing them. Also, you need to keep an eye out for not what only what is there, but what is missing. If we look at the *shinkansen* of JR Tōkai, which operates the Tōkaidō Shinkansen, we see that all of its trains have the same basic colour scheme – white with some form of blue striping. What does this tell us? Using white sends out a signal that the company is hard working and dedicated to good service, since white trains are hard to keep clean. This is something that, of course, may not be apparent to passengers unless trains become dirty, but the message is also being sent to the company's staff who will have the company's ethos drilled into them. The commonality of the colour schemes and the limited designs *shinkansen* operate also reflects the conservatism of the company. Despite being allocated with the corporate colour of orange when JNR was broken up, the colour does not feature on its *shinkansen*, and the company maintains the same basic colour scheme that has been in use since 1964.

Compared to JR Tōkai, we see that JR West, which operates the San'yō Shinkansen, has a much greater variety of rolling stock and use of colours. Although the designs are predominantly the same as would have been found on the Tōkaidō Shinkansen, the length of the trains themselves may be significantly shorter and they may be used for much longer. Both of these facts point to JR West serving smaller cities, where the demand for *shinkansen* is lower than that on the Tōkaidō Shinkansen. We also see that although using the same type of rolling stock as JR Tōkai, JR West will often use a greater variation in colours, although only those that are white with a blue stripe will run through to the Tōkaidō Shinkansen. Looking at the Kyūshū Shinkansen, we can see JR Kyūshū's eye for detail, which has also become a feature of many of their conventional trains. Indeed, the company believes 'good design is good business' (Hood 2006a: 157). So in the *shinkansen* you can find traditional looking bamboo curtains for the windows and *noren* curtains in areas around the toilets. You also see a greater use of wood and more Japanese style patterns on the seats, which vary between carriages. If we turn our attention to JR East, we see that whereas the other companies have one line each, JR East has three main *shinkansen* lines and two mini-*shinkansen* lines. The company faces the challenge of all its services having to use a relatively slow section of train between Tōkyō and Ōmiya and a lack of platforms at Tōkyō station. To help combat this, many services will join together along the route. This also means that shorter trains can be used on sections of the lines, which helps address the fact that much of the network runs through rural areas with smaller cities. But two of the lines also serve major cities on the Kantō plain and the *shinkansen* is used by many commuters. To help respond to this, while keeping in mind the other restrictions mentioned above, JR East developed double-decker *shinkansen*. We also see JR East uses many different colour schemes for its *shinkansen*, with many being specific to services on individual lines, which may even help with passengers identifying the correct service at the crowded Tōkyō platforms.

Of course, we need to remember that there is much more to the Japanese railways than the *shinkansen*. One of the popular images of Japan to demonstrate its crowded nature is the sight of people being pushed and squashed on to trains. There is no doubt that in rush hour, the experience can be particularly unpleasant with little room to move. But is it really that bad compared to the London Underground, where the trains are relatively short on some lines? The problems on British trains, for example, can be compounded by the passengers being reluctant to move along carriages and provide space for people to leave the train at stations. As crowded as Japanese trains are, the degree of cooperation of passengers with each other and the railway company ensures that it is not even worse. As with the *shinkansen*, passengers will queue up at the correct place on the platform, where marks indicate where doors will be on the train, and increasingly this is supported by the use of barriers to ensure that nobody can fall on to the track itself. Companies will even provide diagrams on platforms to inform passengers which carriage they may want to use depending on which exit of a station they may want to use as their destination station.

While there are more to Japanese railways than the *shinkansen*, it is the jewel in the crown of the railways, providing a level of service to which other lines can aspire. It has become a symbol of Japan itself, particularly outside of the country. While it may be obvious to use the image of the *shinkansen* in books or programmes related to travel, an exhibition about experiencing Japan held in London in 2013 also included a picture of a *shinkansen* alongside those of Tōkyō Sky Tree (see Figure 8.1), a robot and the *kanji* for Japan as the only items to feature on promotional material. Thinking back to Exercise 1.1, you may want to think about why these images may have been used, how relevant they remain and the degree to which they are valid, given the development of automation and railways and the size of buildings in some other countries around the world.

BATTLES IN THE SKIES

With punctual, safe trains streaking across the country at speeds of up to 320km/h, you may imagine that there would not be much demand for air travel in Japan. If this is the case, you may be surprised to learn that Japan has 97 airports. In this section, we will look at why there are so many airports and how this ties in with the *shinkansen* network. But before doing that, let us first consider the airlines themselves. Please start by completing Exercise 3.1.

EXERCISE 3.1

How many Japanese airline companies can you name? Do not worry if you struggle with this – this may also be an exercise you will want to try on Japanese people. As you will discover from reading this chapter, paying attention to where in Japan these people come from may also prove illuminating.

When it comes to the Japanese airline companies, Japan Airlines (JAL) is still seen as the national flag carrier. In its time, it has been the largest airline company in the world. However, it has faced a number of challenges, as well as its own internal problems, which combined to leading the company to go bust in one of Japan's largest ever bankruptcies. However, thanks to a combination of internal changes and support from the government, the company turned itself around extremely quickly, and in 2012 was listed in the world's second largest initial public offering (IPO) after Facebook. But rather than JAL, Japan's largest airline company now is All Nippon Airways (ANA). It is perhaps hard to believe that ANA started out as a helicopter company, hence its NH (Nippon Helicopter) flight code, for in April 2013 it had 50 per cent of the domestic market compared to JAL's 27.6 per cent (anna.aero 2013). One problem that remains internationally for ANA is its name. For the company has found that in many countries, as a result of their marketing campaigns for people to visit 'Cool Japan', for example, bookings will go up at Japan Airlines (ANA interview, July 2013).

But the air above Japan has been changing in recent years. Although other companies have existed in Japan, and both JAL and ANA have other affiliated airlines, it was not until 1998 that another airline, Skymark, started to try to really challenge JAL and ANA by introducing lower fares on many of the main routes throughout Japan. However, although its fares were usually lower than ANA and JAL, they were still not comparable to those offered by the newly emerging 'low-cost carriers' (LCCs) in North America and Europe. Today, Skymark has effectively become Japan's third national airline, serving airports across the country, and has also been planning on introducing international services. Skymark is what is often referred to as a 'hybrid carrier', in that it has elements of the service found with legacy carriers such as ANA and JAL, as well as with LCCs. Japan has a number of hybrid carriers now. These include Starflyer (which links northern Kyūshū and Tōkyō's Haneda Airport), Solaseed (which links southern and central Kyūshū with cities across Japan), Air Do (which links cities in Hokkaidō with cities across Japan), Ibex (based in Sendai and serving some smaller routes across the country), and Fuji Dream Airlines (FDA) (based in Shizuoka and Nagoya flying routes across the country).

True LCC operations did not start in Japan until 2012, when three airlines started up within a short time. Two of these, Peach Airlines and AirAsia Japan, were set up partly by ANA, while the third, Jetstar Japan, was partly set up by JAL. Some suggested that LCCs would not be successful in Japan as Japanese prefer to pay higher prices for high-quality goods. This view of the Japanese consumer overlooks the popularity of ¥100 shops and their equivalents, for example. That Japanese people regularly take advantage of the cheap nationwide courier services even when travelling by train or legacy carrier means that the push to limit baggage when taking an LCC is probably less problematic for Japanese than those using LCCs in many European countries, for example.

Even for the casual observer, there are some things that may stand out as puzzling about Japanese airlines. First, let us consider some of the names. We see the names are somehow Japanese without being Japanese. Skymark, for example, cannot be transferred directly in to the phonetic script, and instead comes out as *Sukaimāku*. Solaseed takes its name from the song *do-re-mi*, while also containing a play on '*sora*', the Japanese word for sky and 'sol', the sun. The brand concept is 'seed smiles in the sky' (Solaseed interview, September 2013), whatever that is supposed to mean. However, the name phonetically is actually problematic in Japanese and is rendered as *Sorashido* rather than *Sorashīdo*. Air Do is the brand name of Hokkaidō International Airlines, with the 'Do' being taken from the 'Dō' of Hokkaidō, despite the difference in pronunciation, as well as using the meaning of the English word 'do' to give the impression of action (Air Do interview, August 2013). Peach, while being a popular fruit in Japan and associated with one of the country's most well-known mythical characters (Momotarō), also cannot be rendered into Japanese exactly, but comes out as *Pīchi*. Similarly, ANA's latest flavour of LCC, Vanilla Air, which was established after the joint venture AirAsia Japan turned sour, becomes *Banira Ea*. Why is it that these names have been selected? Of course, names that do not work easily with Japanese phonetics are not limited to airlines, with Sony being *Sonī*, Panasonic being *Panasonikku* and Softbank being *Sofutobanku*. Similarly, Japanese car companies have regularly come up with model names that are either problematic for Japanese phonetics or that have little meaning in English.

Another thing that is noticeable about many of the Japanese airlines is how varied the liveries of the planes can be. Indeed, the variation can be so great that it is sometimes hard to spot which airline's plane it is. The designs may include the use of local characters, pop groups, Disney characters, *manga/anime* characters such as Pokemon (see Figure 3.2), painting the plane so that it looks like an animal, and in the case of one company, FDA, each of its planes are different colours. While the variation in designs is popular with children and those taking photographs, even the airlines do not appear to know whether it leads to any additional sales. So why do it? What does this tell us about Japan? Why is it that we have not seen such variations on the new LCCs? Although JR East has also used Disney characters and Pokemon on its *shinkansen*, for example, it would be hard to imagine them ever being found on JR Tōkai *shinkansen*. So we need to be mindful of the fact that differences in approaches do exist.

Take another look at Figure 3.2 for it also points to another aspect of Japanese domestic travel: the huge numbers of people travelling, or at least the huge numbers travelling on certain routes. This is a specially adapted Boeing 747 'jumbo jet' used for many years in the Japanese market. Each plane can hold up to around 530 passengers, around 200 more than the 747s found on international routes or many other jet planes. Why has Japan used such planes? Because the country is Tōkyō-centric. The main cities of the Kantō plain account for about one-third of the

Figure 3.2 Manga in the skies

country's population. Over one-third of all businesses in Japan have their headquarters in Tōkyō, with the figure being over 60 per cent for those with capital of over ¥100 billion (Fujita and Hill 2005: 18). People and businesses want to be in Tōkyō or connected to Tōkyō. On top of this, the nature of Japan's topography has lent itself to mass public transport. The result is that Haneda-New Chitose is the busiest air sector in the world. Haneda-Itami, Haneda-Fukuoka and Haneda-Okinawa are also in the top 10 (Airline Leader 2013). There is continued pressure to expand Haneda Airport, but with the reintroduction of international services there it is unlikely that smaller regional airports or the LCCs will gain access to the airport. Regional airports and the airlines that serve them are left trying to eke out a business on smaller routes.

The four options for intercity transport, *shinkansen*, legacy airlines, hybrid airlines and LCCs, are largely operating in such a way that there is little direct competition between them. The degree to which any will actually be an option for most Japanese will largely depend on where they live and where they want to get to. But there are exceptions, and the exceptions may point to where better use of taxpayers' money could have been made. Given the Tōkyō-centric nature of long-distance journeys, the consequence is that for areas that are to be included in an expansion of the *shinkansen* network, the case for having a new airport or improvements made to an airport are greatly reduced. And yet, despite plans for the extension of the Hokuriku Shinkansen to Toyama, Kanazawa and beyond, in Ishikawa prefecture Noto Airport was opened in 2003 and improvements were also made to Komatsu Airport. Based on what was seen with plane services after the mini-*shinkansen* lines to Yamagata and Akita, one should expect to see significant cuts to services to the airports along the route of the extended Hokuriku Shinkansen. So why were such airports developed? Or why was the *shinkansen* line developed despite there being airports? There is no single answer to these questions. However, one important aspect has been the influence of politicians, where the desire to help the local economy through large public works projects is a well-known, though perhaps at times exaggerated, part of Japanese politics (Hood 2006b). This 'pork-barrel politics', as it is known, is perhaps a natural development in a democracy where people may be selecting a politician for what he or she will do for their constituency over national concerns. But the implications can stretch beyond the local area. Money that is spent in one area cannot be used in another area, which from a national perspective may have a greater need. In addition to this, with the opening of a new airport, for example, there will be pressure on airlines to provide services to this airport. This pressure was historically particularly placed on JAL due to its national carrier status and the strong links that existed between it and the state through *amakudari* (see Chapter 8). The provision of services on routes for political rather than economic reasons was another of the contributory factors in JAL's bankruptcy and why so many services were slashed as part of its rehabilitation leading to many airports barely having any flights.

Consequently, there appears to be little sign of a coordinated approach to national transportation policies, with the airports and *shinkansen* seen as competitors rather than part of a complementary system. But we need to be careful not to become dragged into thinking in the Tōkyō-centric way of thinking. Airports can aid with connecting cities to not only other cities in Japan where a direct fast rail link is either impractical or impossible, but can also allow for international connections. With the development of LCCs and smaller airlines, as well as more non-Japanese airlines flying to Japan, the private sector may yet provide the ultimate solution to the initial public outlay of money. Although only the JR companies have access to *shinkansen* lines, we need to remember that the lines link cities other than just Tōkyō and may further aid intra- and inter-regional business. Given the environmental challenges that we will be discussing in Chapters 4 and 8, there are also times when more than one option is needed.

EMPTYING THE COUNTRYSIDE

While the previous section may have suggested that the development of airports and the *shinkansen* network may have, on balance, been a positive thing, this section will look at how it may have also helped to accelerate another phenomenon in Japan.

More and more people are choosing to live in larger cities, connected by the *shinkansen* and planes, leading to smaller towns and cities becoming increasingly smaller and the effective shutting down of villages and the countryside.

Before looking at these issues, we should perhaps try to be clear what we mean by the countryside. The Japanese word is *inaka*. However, the nuance of this word is, seemingly for many Japanese, relatively negative and akin to 'backwater' in English. However, the word also appears to be quite nebulous. On travelling on a train in western Tōkyō, I have overheard Japanese passengers, on seeing a few small allotment-like plots of land squeezed among the other houses and buildings, referring to the area as *inaka*. Most children at schools that I taught at in Seto referred to the city as being *inaka*, despite its population of around 120,000 and it being located only 20 km from the centre of Japan's fourth largest city, Nagoya, between which and Seto there is almost no discernable gap in buildings. While many of those who live in larger cities have relations and links to the *inaka* due to the migration that came from these areas in the 1950s and 1960s, many seemingly identify only with their home city, and this has led to a degree of discrimination towards the *inaka*. Indeed, during my first visit to Japan in 1989, I saw a survey on TV that suggested that many city dwellers would not want to marry someone from the *inaka*.

For those who spend their time visiting the larger cities in Japan, it is perhaps difficult to fully appreciate just what the rural areas can be like. I would like to give five examples here as they help to demonstrate some of the challenges being faced by numerous other communities across the country. Ueno–mura, which we will discuss further in Chapter 5, is a village in Gunma prefecture. While many towns and cities have merged, it has kept its village status. While its peak population was 4,854 in 1955 (Uenomura no Chishi Shippitsusha 2003: 46), in 2010 it was just 1,306, ranking it 1,921st out of 1,959 municipalities in Japan (area-info 2014a). While its population is small, its area is not, being approximately the same size as Kawasaki with its population of over 1 million. While much of the village is mountainous and uninhabitable, even the areas where people do live stretch for several kilometres. There are limited shops or other facilities, and for some of the year it can become cut off from the outside world due to the heavy snowfall. But this village is still expected to run and maintain local services, such as the school. Without access to modern conveniences, who will want to live there? What is the impact on prefectural or national finances of maintaining such a village? How are the people supposed to have access to adequate medical care?

If you have seen the James Bond film *You Only Live Twice* (Lewis Gilbert, 1967), you will have seen the small village of Akime, in Kagoshima prefecture (see Figure 3.3). Today, it is relatively easy to visit due to the ease with which Kagoshima can be accessed by plane or *shinkansen*. After that, it is easiest to take a car. There is no regular bus service. A taxi-bus operates at specific times twice a day to Minami-Satsuma, but you have to reserve your place and the return services leave in the early afternoon (Minami-Satsuma-shi 2013). Akime is actually a part of Minami-Satsuma city, but is some 23 km from the city centre. Akime is recognisable from the film that was made over 50 years ago, although the wooden pier has been replaced by a concrete structure, the road is now tarmacked and there is a more developed area for mooring boats protected by a wall and tetrapods (an issue that will be discussed further in Chapter 4). But the village itself barely seems to have changed. Many houses seem to be uninhabited and there are signs that it is only vegetation and wild animals that live here. This is a phenomenon that others such as Matanle (2011) have discussed in relation to other areas in Japan.

You may be thinking that these issues of depopulation may only apply to smaller villages, but they are also impacting larger towns and cities. Let us consider three cities in Nagano that have all been, or will be, impacted by the Hokuriku Shinkansen. This line opened in 1997 in time for the Nagano Olympics. While routes of *shinkansen* lines largely follow those of the conventional lines that already exist, there can be some significant detours to aid with speeding up the journey between larger cities and to reduce construction costs, where a significant factor can be the cost of land in cities, particularly where businesses or people have to be compensated if relocation is required. One city that lost out from the routing of the Hokuriku Shinkansen was Komoro.

Figure 3.3 Akime. Inset shows the memorial stone which was established in 1990 overlooking the bay close to where some of the shots we used in the film were taken.

This former castle city was on the main line between Tōkyō and Nagano and was a popular tourist destination at certain times of the year. Now it has no direct connection to the capital. The rail service is now provided by a joint public and private enterprise that charges higher fares than when the line was operated by JR East, which was allowed to dispose of the loss-making line in lieu of the cost of the *shinkansen* construction. Not only has Komoro seen a dramatic reduction in the number of tourists visiting and an increase in the number of businesses closing down (Hood 2006b: 116), but the population has also gone into decline, from 45,711 in 1995, shortly before the *shinkansen* opened, to 43,997 in 2010 (area-info 2014b). While Komoro was not given direct access to the *shinkansen*, nearby Ueda was. However, a visit there reveals that while the *shinkansen* may have aided with some reconstruction and revitalisation of the city initially, today many shops have closed, leading to the phenomenon of '*shattā-gai*' or 'shutter town' as there are so many shutters down. Iiyama is a city north of Nagano, originally connected to the prefectural capital by a small rural railway line that has sharp turns. However,

Iiyama was included on the route of the Hokuriku Shinkansen. The local government believes that the *shinkansen* station will help to bring in new investment to the city and that tourists will come, particularly in winter thanks to its ski facilities (personal interviews, 2006). However, even before the *shinkansen* station opened the population had crashed from over 27,274 in 2001 to 23,545 in 2010 (area-info 2014c), and I fear that the *shinkansen* will merely accelerate this trend. Although the JR companies themselves point out the benefits of having a *shinkansen* to local governments, which have to cover some of the costs of construction, the reality is that the benefits are likely to be relatively short term, and although those municipalities may be better off than those that do not have stations that were along the original conventional line, the long-term prognosis is poor and the need for trains to stop at these small cities is likely to decrease over time.

Much administration happens at a local, municipal level in Japan. Consequently, with falling populations and falling economic activities in many smaller towns and cities, the finances of local governments have deteriorated. The most well-known example of this was Yubari in Hokkaidō, which declared itself bankrupt in 2007. In an attempt to address these challenges, the government encouraged towns and cities to consider merging with neighbouring municipalities. As a consequence, the number of municipalities had fallen from 3,232 in 1999 to 1,727 in 2010 (Ministry of Internal Affairs and Communications 2010). However, it should be noted that this move was not restricted to smaller cities. For example, the city of Saitama was created through the merger of Ōmiya, Urawa and Yono cities, and subsequently Iwatsuki. You may want to consider what impact such mergers may have also had on people's identities and other issues it may have given rise to. For example, what is the impact upon the people who were born and lived in Tokuyama, which, as part of the process of mergers, has now been renamed as Shūnan but is served still by *shinkansen* and other trains at Tokuyama Station? However, such issues of local identity are presumably not issues for some, for as part of the processes of mergers, one village, Yamaguchi, merged with other towns to become a part of Nakatsugawa, and in the process switched from being Nagano to Gifu prefecture.

The impact of the concentration of Japan's population in larger cities becomes apparent when we look at the cost of land across the country. Figure 3.4 shows the average cost of residential land for each of Japan's 47 prefectures. This figure clearly reveals the huge regional disparities. Here, we need to keep in mind that when land is purchased for residential purposes, having a house standing on that land will often bring the price down further. As many Japanese prefer to have a new house built on a plot of land, the need to tear down an existing building is an additional expense, and so is likely to be reflected in the price they are prepared to pay. In the countryside, many houses have become abandoned as elderly relatives are moved to care homes or die,

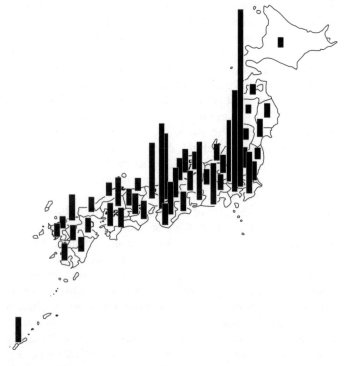

Figure 3.4 Differences in the price of land across Japan

Source of data: MLIT 2014. Height of column is relative to average cost of residential land in the whole prefecture.

and so this is further driving down prices, as well as providing very visual reminders of the run-down nature of many rural areas.

However, the logic for developing the *shinkansen* network was that people could live and work in cities away from the crowded Kantō plain, for example, where land and many other costs were lower. Should there be a need to do business in Tōkyō, for example, the *shinkansen* would provide a fast, punctual and convenient means to get there. However, increasingly it would appear that many Japanese prefer to move to the larger cities and to use the *shinkansen*, or in some cases planes, in order to return to the *furusato*, home town, when necessary. If this trend continues, it means that Japan will see a number of megacities connected by high speed railway lines and by air travel, while in between and around some of the periphery of the country there will be almost nobody living save a few needed to provide agricultural or tourist services, but the quality of their lives will be severely impacted by the lack of sustainability of many other services. But before this trend reaches its conclusion, there are issues to be addressed.

MODERN *UBASUTEYAMA*

One of Japan's more infamous legends is of *ubasuteyama*, whereby elderly or infirm relatives were apparently taken to a place such as a mountain (*yama*) and abandoned. The degree to which it was widely practised is debatable, but it is a concept that has led to a range of stories and poems. Is Japan today creating a form of *ubasuteyama*?

Although not condemned to death, the elderly are seemingly increasingly left in villages in rural areas. These villages do not have the medical provision that larger towns and cities would have. These grandparents are away from their younger relatives, when only a few decades ago it was still common for three generations of a family to live together in a single house. Such families are still seen in other Asian nations such as China and Hong Kong, so why is it that the move to urbanisation and economic prosperity has seen this shift in Japan?

Of course, not all old people in Japan live in the countryside; there are many in the cities too. But even there, many will live in their own accommodation, or increasingly in care homes. The issue is one that has grown in scale in recent years due to two phenomena: the increasing life expectancy of the Japanese and the impact of the 'baby boom' after the Second World War. The average life expectancy for women born in 2012 was 86.4 years, which was the highest in the world, whereas it was 79.9 years for men (Ministry of Internal Affairs and Communications 2013: 20). In 2012, the number of Japanese aged 100 or over reached 51,376, compared to just 153 in 1963 (Nenji-toukei 2014a). The consequence is that Japan now has the challenge of how to support a large retired population with a relatively small and decreasing workforce. As the baby boomers gradually die, the size of the challenge will alter, and the Japanese government has been looking at ways to address both the current and long-term challenges. As the retired require pensions, and often additional medical treatment, there is a need to increase tax revenues to cover these costs or to find ways of reducing the government contribution to these costs. Raising taxes is rarely popular, regardless of the logic of why the move may be necessary, and many Japanese governments since the 1980s have had problems with introducing and raising the consumption tax, a form of value added tax seen in many other countries, to help cover the increasing costs.

The longer lifespans of many Japanese has led to situations whereby upon reaching retirement, it is not uncommon to be looking after one's parents or parents-in-law rather than being supported by one's own children. But it would be wrong to present an overly negative picture. Many of the retired population are fit and well. While in Chapter 2 we discussed the importance of female consumers, it should be of no surprise that the retired are also an important market. While many retirees may have a tendency to save to help cover medical costs that may escalate, there are many who also spend. Travel is particularly popular, and so many companies have developed strategies to target this market. Discount fares are offered by many rail companies, while the LCCs also believe that they will be an attractive option for these cost-conscious consumers. Keeping in mind how active many of the retired Japanese are reveals why it is important to avoid discussing the size of the 'greying population' as a *problem*.

The focus for many years now has been on the need to develop a more 'barrier-free' society. Whereas in public there has been support for those with sight disabilities in particular, for example through the provision of yellow markers on pavements, brail at many public buildings and stations, and audible alerts at pedestrian crossings, the focus has moved to making Japan more accessible to those with more physical challenges. In public places, this has seen a shift to improving access for wheelchairs, for example. Of course, some of these moves have a broader impact. With it now being compulsory for all stations in Tōkyō to have lifts, it is noticeable how there are many more parents using prams than in the past. Indeed, it is more common to see prams than wheelchairs on public transport, whatever the original motivation was for the policy. Whereas the installation of lifts was a major financial burden for railway companies, for which there was some support from the state, we need to remember the benefit it would have brought for many lift manufacturers. Indeed, the increase in retired people in Japan has also led to opportunities for some companies who have been developing products and ranges that take account of the differing needs and requirements of older consumers.

SUMMARY

In this chapter, we have taken journeys across Japan looking at the operation of the *shinkansen* and the development of the domestic airline industry. The chapter has pointed out a number of features that can be learnt about Japan through looking at the transportation system, but has also emphasised the impact that the apparent improvements in intercity transport have had and that, particularly with the Japanese population falling and more people seemingly wanting to live in large cities, the improvements may be accelerating a process of emptying out the countryside. The chapter then pointed out how these changes are likely to be particularly significant in relation to Japan's retired population.

4

NATURAL JAPAN

Japan is quiet. It is a country that is often associated with the peace and tranquillity of temple gardens, Zen meditation and the stunning natural beauty of its mountains. I expect that your answers to Exercise 1.1 may have included some of these apparent natural or peaceful symbols of Japan. But how representative are these symbols and what do they really tell us about the country we are studying? In this chapter, we will explore a number of these symbols and consider Japan's environmental record. This chapter will highlight some themes that have already begun to surface in the previous chapters, in particular the battle between local and national interests, the significance of commercial interests and questions about who creates Japan's national symbols. Is it the Japanese or the outsiders?

HERITAGE SITES

Let us begin by returning to the image in Figure 3.1. While Chapter 3 considered the *shinkansen*, we have not looked in detail at the other important component of the picture: Mount Fuji. At 3,776m, the conical shape of Mount Fuji is an impressive site and is one that has inspired poetry, artwork and photography throughout Japan's history. Although far from one of Asia's tallest mountains or one of the world's tallest mountains, its distinctive shape, often snow-capped peak and the fact that it stands away from many other mountains, enabling so much of its height to be visible from its base, makes it an impressive sight.

On a clear day, Mount Fuji is clearly visible from Tōkyō, despite being some 100 km away. The number of days on which Mount Fuji is visible from Tōkyō has varied over the years. During most years in the 1960s, it was visible between 40 and 50 times per year, by the end of the 1980s it was unusual for there to be more than 40 days per year, and in 1987 there were just 20 (Tōkyō Metropolitan Government 2013). With observations done from a new, taller building since 1992, comparisons become more diffi-cult, but even between that year when there were 84 observations we see that there has seemingly been an improvement, with observations being possible on 95 or more days in 2010, 2011 and 2012 (Tōkyō Metropolitan Government 2013). Ironically, it is often hard to see Mount Fuji from the *shinkansen* as it can become obscured by clouds, some of which are formed due in part it seems to a large number of paper mills spewing out steam around its base. Many wishing to see or visit Mount Fuji will go to its northern side, which has lakes, tourist facilities and even one of Japan's largest theme parks. We will discuss this side of Mount Fuji further in the next chapter.

Although it is Japan's tallest mountain, it is not as challenging as many of Japan's other mountains to climb, such as Mount Tanigawa (1,977m) (see Figure 4.1), which claims many lives each year and is claimed by many Japanese to have more deaths than any other mountain in the world, while it remains relatively unknown in the English-speaking world. The number climbing Mount Fuji has also risen in recent years, from 200,292 in 2005 to a peak of 320,975 in 2010 (Ministry of the Environment 2013). Most visitors will not climb the whole mountain, but will take a road to Gogome, 'the fifth station', and then take one of the climbing routes from there. No special climbing equipment is needed, and this climb is 1,471m. The other 'stations' during the climb are much smaller than Gogome, but some have accom-modation where visitors can sleep overnight, allowing them to wake in time to get to the peak for sunrise.

Figure 4.1 Mount Tanigawa. In the foreground a school trip approach the towering Ichinokura-sawa face of Mount Tanigawa, towering some 330m above them.

But the number of visitors to Mount Fuji has brought its own problems, particularly rubbish. Although efforts have been made to keep the mountain clean, the large number of visitors has made this a challenge and led to a fee of ¥1,000 to climb Mount Fuji to be introduced from 2014 (Japan Today, 26 December 2013). One of the factors that also helped inspire this drive to keep Mount Fuji clean was that in 2013, the mountain was awarded UNESCO World Heritage Site status. But why is it that, when we have discussed the cooperation of passengers in the previous chapter in relation to boarding trains, climbers seem unable to cooperate and take their own rubbish off Mount Fuji with them?

Mount Fuji is not Japan's only UNESCO World Heritage Site, as can be seen from Table 4.1, which lists all of those awarded this status up to 2013 in order of the year awarded. Table 4.1 should lead you to ask a number of questions, for example: Why does Japan want these sites to have this status? Why were these sites selected? Why were the sites selected in the order that they were? What sites are not on the list that you may have expected to be on the list? Are efforts being made to have these sites added to the list? Does the awarding of UNESCO World Heritage Site status significantly boost visitor numbers? If so, does this have a positive or negative impact on sites that do not have UNESCO World Heritage Site status? You may also want to find out what, if any, UNESCO World Heritage Sites there are in your own country for comparison.

Table 4.1 Japan's UNESCO World Heritage Sites

Place	Location	Year awarded status
Himeji Castle	Hyōgo	1993
Shirakami-Sanchi	Aomori/Akita	1993
Yakushima	Kagoshima	1993
Historic Monuments of Ancient Kyōto (Kyōto, Uji and Ōtsu Cities)	Kyōto and Shiga	1994
Historic Villages of Shirakawa-go and Gokayama	Gifu/Toyama	1995
Hiroshima Peace Memorial (Genbaku Dome)	Hiroshima	1996
Itsukushima Shinto Shrine	Hiroshima	1996
Historic Monuments of Ancient Nara	Nara	1998
Buddhist Monuments in the Horyū-ji Area	Nara	1999
Shrines and Temples of Nikkō	Tochigi	1999
Gusuku Sites and Related Properties of the Kingdom of Ryukyu	Okinawa	2000
Sacred Sites and Pilgrimage Routes in the Kii Mountain Range	Mie/Nara/ Wakayama	2004
Shiretoko	Hokkaidō	2005
Iwami Ginzan Silver Mine and its Cultural Landscape	Shimane	2007
Hiraizumi – Temples, Gardens and Archaeological Sites Representing the Buddhist Pure Land	Iwate	2011
Ogasawara Islands	Tōkyō	2011
Mount Fuji	Shizuoka/ Yamanashi	2013

Source: Table by the author based on information from UNESCO (2013).

As mentioned above, the awarding of UNESCO World Heritage Site status means that there has to be a commitment to maintain the upkeep of the site. This means that consideration has to be given to who will do this, which will almost certainly involve a cost. But who will bear this cost? The answer to this relates to ownership of the site. Perhaps few who look at or visit Mount Fuji would stop to consider who owns it. That its ownership is problematic may come as a surprise, then (Japan Today, 9 February 2014). But Mount Fuji is not the only place in Japan where there are boundary and ownership issues. For example, Lake Towada was the subject of a dispute between Akita and Aomori prefectures that was not settled until 2008. Perhaps Japan's most infamous ownership issues relate to islands where other countries also claim ownership, but we will discuss these further in Chapter 6.

CONTROLLING AND IMPACTING NATURE

Looking back at your list from Exercise 1.1, how many 'natural' symbols do you have listed? As well as Mount Fuji, Japan is also associated with its gardens, snowy landscapes in some parts of the country during winter, and a range of wildlife. Japanese and visitors alike will often seek out these sites for themselves. But such tourism is not without its problems. Already, we have discussed the problems of rubbish when the number of visitors increases. But we also need to think about access. While Japan may have an extensive high-speed railway network and numerous airports, these may not directly serve tourist destinations. Additional railways and roads, in particular, are likely to be needed. Increased numbers of visitors will mean increased traffic, which will mean increased congestion and pollution and problems for local residents. One also has to wonder what additional impacts there may be.

The Yudanaka Jigokudani, or 'Monkey Park' as it is somewhat simplistically referred to in English, is home to one of the most well-used images of Japan's nature, for it is home to the macaques that are famed for entering *onsen* (hot springs). This sight is particularly of interest it seems and aesthetically pleasing during winter when surrounded by snow (see Figure 4.2). But how natural is this? Of all the pictures that I took during my most recent visit, I had to consider which one to use in this book. Should I use one that concentrates on the macaques or one that also shows the number of visitors standing around watching and photographing like me? Which one of these situations is the more natural? Although undoubtedly the day on which I visited had some impact, the number of visitors on my visit in 2014 was much greater than the one I made in 1997. However, during both visits a foreign television camera crew were present. During my most recent visit, the number of non-Japanese visitors was very evident. I dare say that the more the images of these macaques appear in books and on television programmes, the more visitors to Japan will seek out this location for themselves. The site also has a webcam so people do not have to leave the comfort of their homes to see how the animals behave. But what should we be watching? Should we be watching the macaques or the humans? Who is like whom? Watching the macaques, it is easy to see things that make you think how human they are – but saying humans are like macaques may be just as fitting. Why is that we try to look for similarities between humans and

Figure 4.2 Bathing macaques surrounded by snow

macaques, but then focus on trying to find the differences between humans and other humans, Japanese and non-Japanese?

Comparing my two visits, it appears that the number of macaques has swelled and I suspect that the provision of food in the harsh conditions is one factor in this. As before, they seemed unconcerned about the humans around them most of the time, and they do not interact with the humans, walking past them, or indeed over them, if they are sat taking photographs. It was also noticeable during my second visit that a number left the *onsen* when they needed to relieve themselves, with their mess quickly cleared by one of the people who maintain the site. Is this some form of evolving concern about cleanliness or are there other factors driving it? Sitting in their man-made pool with naturally hot water being piped in, the dividing line between natural and constructed remains blurred.

There is no doubt that there is much natural beauty in Japan. However, in the end one cannot escape the human interaction with it. Buruma (2001: 65) argues that the Japanese love of nature is 'tinged with a deep fear of the unpredictable forces that it can unleash', which we will discuss in Chapter 8, and that this leads to 'abhorrence' to 'nature in the raw'. Perhaps Buruma's view is extreme, but one cannot deny that almost wherever one looks there is evidence of how many Japanese have made attempts to control and restrict nature. While nature is something that is to be respected and even worshipped, as we will discuss in the next chapter, that does not mean that nature is simply left alone to do as it wishes. Look again at Figure 3.3. Even in this remote small village, you can see the scars of humanity's impact on the local environment, from the use of tarmac on the roads, to the use of concrete harbour walls, to the seemingly ubiquitous sight around Japan's coastline of concrete tetrapods to provide additional protection. These appear to be signs of a contemporary version of Japan's 'iron triangle' that links the politicians, the bureaucracy and construction industry, which has led to Japan being referred to as a 'construction state' (e.g. Kingston 2012: 194). Of course, if you go looking you are likely to see similar sights in developed countries around the world – albeit in some countries there may be greater attempts to beautify such 'improvements' by using concrete shaped as rocks. You may think that the elevated sections and bridges of the *shinkansen* lines rarely have the aesthetic qualities of the Victorian constructions found in Britain, but is that a reflection of how we have come to define man-made beauty and a lack of respect for functional simplicity? It is easy to criticise the visual impact of concrete that one sees across Japan when visiting, but it is just as easy to not be aware of the impact if such measures were not taken. Would a Japanese person be impressed by the lack of concrete seemingly evident along Britain's coastline or along the riverbanks and riverbeds akin to what would be found in Japan? Would Japanese people applaud the way in which many British rivers have seemingly been left to fill up with silt − whether for natural or economic reasons? How many would have seen the news of the impact on swathes of communities of floods in Britain in 2014? While this is as much a question about what the Japanese media reports as what the Japanese people themselves take an interest in, consider the question the other way around. How likely is it that the news in your country would show images of floods in Japan? If it was a large, single event, perhaps, as this is what may be termed a disaster, but smaller, more regular occurrences are not likely to feature. How do we then put a price, economic or otherwise, on the desire to protect communities from nature?

But attempts to control nature do not always have to be on such a large scale, or to do with holding back its impact on humans. Japan is famed for its gardens. But as we discussed in Chapter 2, most Japanese homes have limited space for gardens of their own (see Figure 2.3), and so when we discuss Japanese gardens we tend to be focusing on those found at shrines and other public locations. While the rocks, stones and plants are natural, the way in which they are placed, allowed to grow and maintained reveals a very precise degree of planning and level of control. Of course, this is true of gardens around the world. Referring back to Buruma, does the fact that such gardens exist reveal a love or abhorrence of nature? Is *bonsai* an art form necessitated by a lack of space or a means for humans to feel in control over and belittle nature?

While so far we have discussed the steps that may be taken to control or limit nature and the environment, there are also times when there is an impact upon the surroundings, although it may not always become an area for concern until it impacts humans. Earlier in this chapter, we touched upon environmental issues in relation to the problems of seeing Mount Fuji from Tōkyō, but there are many other environmental problems that could be discussed. The history of these problems goes in parallel with Japan's economic development and modernisation. The expansion of factories, many of which are close to residential areas rather than in industrial zones, that helped drive Japan's rapid economic expansion during the 1950s and 1960s brought new challenges. The drive for economic improvements was seemingly done without much concern for the physical and mental well-being of its people, let alone the impact it was having on the natural habitat.

Problems of pollution first became evident in major cities such as Kawasaki, Yokkaichi and Kitakyūshū, where the bay was declared dead and void of all fish, for example. In time, new environmental laws were passed, and today the water is again blue in Kitakyūshū and fish live there once more (Institute for Global Environmental Strategies 2013), although some of the improvement may have also been aided in the shift in production to other countries too. However, discussion of environmental pollution in Japan will always be synonymous with one city: Minamata. As early as 1953, some people in the city had begun to complain about a strange disease, which in time would come to be referred to as 'Minamata-*byō*' ('Minamata Disease'). However, the problems, which included numbness, muscular spasms and problems speaking, were not due to a disease, as it could not be caught from other sufferers, but through ingestion of a chemical, methyl mercury, which had seemingly been released into the water supply by Chisso, a large company in the city. Arguably, it was not until photographs taken by a non-Japanese, Eugene Smith, raised international awareness of the problem in the 1970s (Bauer 2006: 122), by which time children were being born with deformities and many people were crippled or had died. While some compensation was given out, the amounts were pitifully low and not all received it. Only then did the government begin to take any action. However, the degree to which it acted and compensated the victims remains an ongoing issue and one that you should research further. However, in doing so, there are issues you may want to keep in mind that highlight the problems of environmental law and the balance between local and economic demands and the impact on victims. If it was methyl mercury in the local water that was the problem, why did all locals not suffer the same symptoms? To what degree should a company compensate? What if the level of compensation meant that the company was no longer able to operate? As the largest employer in the area, the impact on the local economy through the loss of jobs initially and then the knock-on effect of the reduced spending by these former Chisso employees in other shops and restaurants, for example, could devastate the area further. Is this why so few did seek compensation and action in the early years especially?

The balance between local demands and national needs also gets played out in relation to one issue that has become the attention of the world since 2011 in particular. In part as a result of the tsunami triggered by the Great East Japan Earthquake, the Fukushima Dai-ichi Nuclear Power Station was damaged, leading to a meltdown in three of its four reactors and the release of radiation. The reason why I say that this was 'in part' a result of the earthquake and tsunami will be discussed in Chapter 8. Here, let us focus upon why Japan, given that it is in an area of the planet where there are many earthquakes, has nuclear power stations and why they are where they are.

As we have mentioned in Chapter 2, Japan has limited natural resources of its own. As demands for power increase, so more has needed to be imported. While vehicles have not had any alternative to petrol and diesel, to produce electricity there are alternatives, including nuclear power. So it was that not even 10 years after suffering the atomic attacks on Hiroshima and Nagasaki, Japan decided to embrace nuclear power and commissioned its first nuclear power station (World Nuclear Association 2014). By 2011, nuclear power accounted for nearly one-third of all electricity generated (World Nuclear Association 2014). Following the events in Fukushima in 2011 and the fact that this exposed problems within the safety culture in the Japanese nuclear industry again, as will be discussed in Chapter 8, all the nuclear power stations were switched off. The question as to what will happen to the nuclear power stations in Japan returns in part to the question as to why the nuclear power stations are where they are. Think back to Chapter 3 and how we have discussed the challenges facing rural areas. Having a nuclear power station would bring construction jobs as well as long-term employment prospects (Dusinberre 2012). The question is not so much whether these villages and towns would want a nuclear power station, but why would they not want one? Then, similar to Chisso in Minamata, as the power stations are often the largest employer, there are local demands to have the power stations turned back on now. The alternative for these communities could be devastating. That it is the local mayor that makes the final decision to accept or refuse the power company's request to restart the power station after additional safety checks are completed in the wake of the events at Fukushima means that local demands rather than national policies could end up deciding what happens.

There are also significant economic demands that are driving the debate about power supply. Think back to Exercise 2.1 and how exchange rates impact prices. If Japan imports more fossil fuels to compensate for the lack of nuclear power, it needs the exchange rate to drop so that the cost of the fuels becomes cheaper to import. However, this then means that Japanese goods, assuming their yen price does not alter, will become more expensive for other countries to import. Keep in mind that there are Japanese companies that also sell components to other companies that produce the final product. For example, there are Japanese companies that supply parts that make up significant proportions of the Boeing 787 Dreamliner and also Apple's iPads and iPhones. Putting aside the usual pricing strategies of these companies, they will have faced pressure to raise their prices due to the relative increase in the price of the imported Japanese components unless an agreed price in dollars had been negotiated, in which case the Japanese company would be left facing a much reduced income. One can imagine that Japan's exporters would be pressuring the government to intervene so that the exchange rate may be more favourable to them. This in turn would mean that pressure to turn back on the nuclear power stations would increase. Meanwhile, as the prospect for new nuclear power stations to be approved are limited, for Japanese companies involved in the nuclear industry, the pressure to look for markets outside Japan will also increase.

Are there alternatives to nuclear power? Two main options are alternative power sources or reducing the demand for electricity. For years, alternative energy has not been seen as a viable option in Japan, despite the fact that many Japanese companies are significant players in the development and selling of solar cells and panels, as well as turbines for wind power, for example. While the number of wind farms had been increasing significantly up to 2011, since then, despite the fact that all of the wind farms in the affected area withstood the earthquake and tsunami, the increases in wind power have been more modest. New procedures have been introduced to look at the environmental impact of new construction (JWPA 2014). One has to wonder what, or who, was the real motivating force for this. In relation to solar power in Japan, space is often a major constraint. Many station and airport buildings, for example, have had solar panels installed on their roofs, and loss-making Makurazaki Airport was closed in 2012 to become a large solar power plant. While renewable energy, including hydroelectric, accounted for about 10 per cent in 2011, the target is for this to rise to 20 per cent. Originally the target was for this to be met by 2030, but nuclear problems have brought this forward by 10 years (*The Japan Times*, 27 May 2011). In the meantime, the pressure to reduce electricity usage remains.

'*Setsuden*' is the Japanese word to refer to the policy of reducing electricity consumption in light of the increased costs and reduced supplies following the suspension of the nuclear power stations. Signs appeared across Japan encouraging people to reduce their electricity consumption, although none as ironic as when Japan last faced an energy crisis. In 1973, as a consequence of the oil crisis, one skyscraper in Shinjuku kept some lights on all night so that it spelt out the *kanji* for *setsuden* (Horsley and Buckley 1990: 115). While people are encouraged to reduce their power consumption, companies have had to take more proactive steps. So, for example, on trains many companies removed alternative strip lights, making carriages darker but generally still light enough, and many companies set air conditioners to a higher temperature setting so that they did not need to be used so much. If anything, this was an improvement as it removed the significant temperature variations between air-conditioned facilities and the outside, which tended to exaggerate the heat when it was necessary to venture outside. Indeed, in such cases, is this not reducing electricity wastage rather than merely reducing electricity demand? Other examples of *setsuden* would suggest that the policy was not always properly thought through; for example, some drinks machines provided drinks that were warm, while others merely had the lighting turned off or reduced. As time has gone by, the signs of *setsuden* being implemented have reduced. Is this because people have said that they would rather pay more and keep certain services? Or is it that other improvements are starting to be made in the design of products that use electricity?

RESPONDING TO NATURAL CHALLENGES

Japan's relationship with the environment is not one way. As well as impacting upon the environment in certain areas, there are times when aspects of daily life have to respond to natural challenges. Perhaps the greatest of these are earthquakes and tsunami, which we will discuss in Chapter 8. However, there are other areas too, and we can look at some of these through how it impacts upon the operations of the *shinkansen*.

For the *shinkansen*, perhaps the greatest natural challenge it faces is Japan's topography. As we have discussed before, the country is very mountainous. As trains operate most effectively on level tracks, it is usually necessary to either go around mountains or go through them via tunnels. Although many of Japan's conventional railways do go around mountains, this leads to many bends and slows services down. Clearly, for the *shinkansen* this would not be an option, and so it has been necessary to build numerous tunnels. However, these tunnels have produced a further challenge. Due to the speed at which the *shinkansen* travel, a pressure wave builds up when the train enters a tunnel, which can lead to a loud noise as the train exits the tunnel (RTRI and EJRCF 2001: 125). With housing often being found near tracks on some lines such as the San'yō Shinkansen, there have been demands to try to reduce the impact on the residents. While more aerodynamic designs of trains have helped, companies such as JR West have constructed hoods with slats in the roof, which are effective in reducing the impact of the pressure waves.

Line side noise pollution has been an issue since the early years of the *shinkansen* and has grown due to the increased urbanisation so that more and more housing has been constructed near lines. Environmental laws introduced in the 1970s meant that new lines had to have walls that would limit the amount of noise escaping from the line (Hood 2006a: 174). The development of lighter trains has also helped reduce the amount of noise produced by the train over time. However, for those living near the line, particularly the elevated sections, the sound of the *shinkansen* remains very noticeable. The elevated sections have been developed to address two issues. First, it means that there is no need for level crossings or road bridges. Second, it ensures that the need for variations in the height of the railway line and slopes are reduced. However, elevated sections not only tend to lead to noise pollution, but they are also particularly unsightly. While this is not obvious as you travel around the country on *shinkansen*, for those living in the cities where it passes through, it is hard to avoid, as in some locations the construction may be as high as a six-storey building. Even when there is no train, the line is always there.

It should perhaps be of no surprise that not all Japanese have been in favour of the development of the *shinkansen* network due to the impact it can have on the local environment. In most cases, the construction has gone ahead through the payment of compensation to those affected, such as when people have had to move homes so that their house could be destroyed to make way for a new line. As land prices increased, the level of compensation also increased, and this is an issue for any construction in and around Tōkyō in particular (see Chapter 3). Although dealing with the opponents of the *shinkansen* line construction between Ōmiya and Ueno was particularly problematic (see Groth 1996), nothing compares to the level of protests relating to the construction and expansion of Narita Airport. The opposition was so great that those on the committee that handled compulsory purchase applications had their homes attacked, which led to the members resigning. As no new people agreed to join the committee, the work of the committee could not be done (Hood 2006a: 86). This issue dates back to the 1970s, but its impact can still be seen in the form of a house that has had to be built around in the middle of the taxiways at the airport.

Clearly, the noise pollution created by transportation is not an issue for all in Japan. Indeed, noise pollution rarely seems to be a concern in Japan. While one of the images of Japan may come from the tranquillity of its Zen temples or Japanese gardens, the reality is that background music is found almost everywhere. Walking down many streets, there will also be the shrill emanating from pachinko parlours. Most TV programmes and adverts will also have accompanying music – usually with the name of the track on display to aid those who may want to purchase it. Even in the countryside when there are seemingly hardly any people around, I have experienced the disturbance caused by politicians campaigning for election by shouting out slogans across megaphones on more than one occasion.

In the previous section, we discussed the need to try to reduce electricity consumption. While reduction is a key concept in improving environmental performance, another is recycling. In relation to the *shinkansen*, we see recycling in two main areas. The first relates to the construction of the train itself where companies have been looking to increase the proportion of the train that can be recycled when it comes to break up a train after it has been withdrawn from service (Hood 2006a: 173). The second area relates to encouraging passengers to recycle as much of their rubbish as possible. Trains and platforms have separate bins (bottles, cans, PET bottles, newspaper/magazines and 'others') to encourage environmentally responsible behaviour. Of course, the separation of rubbish is something that also happens at home. That people will sort out their rubbish on a train or at home further illustrates how odd it is that so many will leave rubbish lying around on Mount Fuji, for example.

Another natural challenge that the *shinkansen* faces is the weather. Due to the location and length of the country, the weather can vary greatly from season to season and be very different at any particular time. Indeed, the start and finish dates of seasons are not fixed. Rather, the Meteorological Agency will announce when winter, for example, has started due to certain weather patterns being observed. However, this will be done on a regional basis so that it is possible for two or more seasons being experienced by different parts of Japan at any given time. Even when different parts of Japan are in winter, for example, the nature of winter can vary from region to region. On the east coast, snow will tend to be lighter than the wetter, heavier snow found on the Japan Sea coast. For the *shinkansen*, these differences are significant in trying to maintain punctual services. On the east coast, the pressure wave, which can be such a problem in noise pollution, is effective in blowing the snow out of the way. For the lines passing through the areas where heavier snow falls, the pressure wave is not sufficient, and so sprinklers are employed to melt the falling snow (Hood 2006a: 165–6). Consequently, snow is rarely a problem these days for the *shinkansen*, although maintaining a punctual service clearly comes at a price. Keeping airports operating during the winter can be more problematic, and so airlines, such as Air Do, which serve Hokkaidō in particular will often see their services impacted (Air Do interview, August 2013).

While it is possible to develop countermeasures to help the *shinkansen* deal with snow, it is not so easy to respond to the challenges presented by rain. To help understand the scale of the challenge, please complete Exercise 4.1.

You will see that rainfall in Japan is particularly high in June as this is when 'rainy season' tends to be, which could be considered as an extra season in addition to the four main seasons. Due to the heavy rainfall and topography of Japan, landslides can be a particular problem (Noguchi and Fujii 2000: 52). To help counter this, many hillsides are covered with concrete. Although historically these concrete scars were very visible, recently the designs have changed so that in time they often become covered with vegetation so that they cannot be seen. As with coastal defences, which we discussed above, while the concrete can be unsightly, you need to think about how to balance these concerns with the potential devastating impact if such measures are not taken. But you should also think about the broader impact of the measures: Where do the materials come from? How much does it cost? Who benefits financially from such construction work? What is the decision-making process involved in deciding where such measures are employed?

While there are undoubtedly many challenges presented to the Japanese by the weather, it also leads to many business opportunities. The heat and humidity may be uncomfortable, but for companies developing air conditioners it is a sales opportunity. The

---

EXERCISE 4.1

Using a resource such as www.climatemps.com/, find out what the average precipitation in each month is for the following cities across Japan and for a number of cities around the world. If the city you live in is not listed, then you may want to look this up too. You may also want to look at the typical average temperature for each month.

	Sapporo	Tōkyō	Ōsaka	Naha	London	New York	Sydney
January							
February							
March							
April							
May							
June							
July							
August							
September							
October							
November							
December							

---

electricity companies in turn make money from the use of the air conditioners. With a need to reduce electricity consumption, the desire to replace machines with more efficient ones is a further business opportunity, although one has to think about what happens to the disposed machinery. That seasons happen at different times is also a business opportunity, particularly for the travel industry, as people will often travel to go to experience the sights and flavours associated with regional, seasonal specialities.

NATURAL FOOD

It is possible that when you completed Exercise 1.1, you included Japanese food or particular examples of Japanese food as some symbols of Japan. Indeed, the Japanese government has even been seeking to have Japanese food recognised for its distinctiveness by UNESCO. However, there are many things to consider in relation to Japan's food culture, particularly when we are still thinking about environmental issues in this chapter. In the previous section, mention was given to the different types of bins that are found on trains and at stations. Part of the need for the increase in bins has been the shift to people using *bentō* (lunch boxes), with the regional speciality type ones found at stations (*ekiben*) being particularly popular. We could also look at the significance of sushi and even how its increased popularity around the world has impacted upon the stocks of tuna in particular and the price that a single fish can reach. However, when it comes to Japan and food, the most infamous ingredient is whale meat.

In relation to whaling and Japan, it is worth reflecting upon the following sentence, which appears in *Moby Dick*: 'If that double-bolted land, Japan, is ever to become hospitable, it is the whale-ship alone to whom the credit will be due; for already she is on the threshold' (Melville 1851: 110). Within that sentence are two points that are noteworthy. First, as the book was published in 1851, before Japan opened up from its period of seclusion, it would appear that the conditions in Japan were perhaps more known about than we may expect, and so we have to question the degree to which the seclusion was as strict as is sometimes portrayed. Second, the sentence points to the fact that whaling was not seen as so unacceptable to countries such as the United States, as it appears to be today. Given the complexity of the issue and how emotive it can be, here I would like to alert you to certain key points and get you to think about certain questions that you should consider as you continue your study of Japan.

There are many different types of whales, with the two main categories being baleen, which feed on krill and small fish, and toothed, which feed on squid, fish and other animals. Typically, in English those types that grow to over 4m in length are referred to as whales, while the others are referred to as dolphins or porpoises. Although Japanese also has a separate word for each type of whale, whales themselves are referred to as *kujira*. The *kanji* for *kujira* (鯨), like most *kanji*, is made up through a combination of other *kanji*, with one part, referred to as a 'radical', pointing to its inherent meaning. The radical for *kujira* is the left-hand side of the *kanji* and is the *kanji* for *sakana* (魚), fish. On this basis, a whale is fundamentally a fish rather than being first and foremost a mammal. Of course, even in countries where there may be criticism for Japan's killing of these mammals, many other mammals, such as cows and pigs, may be killed for consumption. With beef and pork not eaten by those who follow particular religions, let alone the fact there are many vegetarians, should the killing of cattle and pigs be stopped? This may be unimaginable in many countries. If so, can we really expect outside pressure to lead to Japan changing its food culture and stopping whaling?

Rather than merely the fact of killing whales for their meat, arguments that whales are intelligent animals or endangered are also put forward as to why they should not be killed. However, even the International Whaling Commission (IWC), which was originally set up for countries to regulate whaling but has now taken on a conservation agenda, suggests that there are significant numbers of most types of whales – particularly those such as Minke, which Japanese whalers have tended to catch for consumption (IWC 2014a). The IWC allows for some whales to be captured for 'aboriginal subsistence' in countries such as Greenland and even the USA (IWC 2014b). So why does Japan not apply to catch some whales on this basis? Until 2014, it had caught whales for 'research' despite the suspicion that the meat was destined for human consumption. In 2014, the 'World Court' banned Japan from conducting this type of whaling in the South Pacific. So what will Japan do next? Why has Japan apparently encouraged many small non-whaling nations to join the IWC to support its position in return for other aid? Why does Japan not just leave the IWC, as Iceland has done, and continue its whaling as it wishes? Why does the media focus so much on Japanese?

The irony of the whaling debate in relation to Japan is that not only was whaling one of the reasons why the United States was keen for Japan to end its period of seclusion so that it could have access to its ports for whaling ships to refuel (Jansen 2009: 274), but it was also the American occupation government that encouraged Japan to capture whales for consumption when other foods were in short supply following the Second World War

(Russell 2004: 80). But today, although specialist whale meat restaurants do exist and some shops sell its meat, whale meat has become something that many Japanese rarely, if ever, eat. While it may be served occasionally for school lunches in some parts of Japan, whale meat is far from being part of the typical diet. This has led to stockpiles of frozen whale meat building up over the past decade (Japan Today, 30 March 2014). So why has the Japanese government been so prepared to face international criticism over the issue? Is it to support the few, small remaining communities that apparently rely on whaling? Why would it be so important to protect these jobs?

One of the cities that is home to whaling vessels is Taiji. However, while some protest at the methods needed to kill larger whales, Taiji is also associated with the killing of smaller whales, specifically dolphins, and became the subject of the documentary film *The Cove* (Louie Psihoyos, 2009). Dolphins are driven into a cove where they are captured so that they may be sold to water parks around both Japan and the world. But those making the documentary are not Japanese. Those that protest about both whaling in general and about what takes place in Taiji also tend not to be Japanese. Why is there seemingly so little protest by Japanese people? Why does the Japanese media not discuss what takes place in Taiji? Is it because once there is an acceptance that something can be killed or captured, the conditions or how it happens are not considered an issue? Is this why many Japanese farmers are prepared to keep cows in sheds like battery hens? Is it why the eating of some fish while they are still alive, for example peeling parts of the body off a cuttlefish for *sashimi*, is not seen as cruel?

SUMMARY

This chapter has taken a number of images relating to natural Japan and looked at how they reveal different aspects of Japanese society. This chapter has considered the symbolic importance of Mount Fuji and how it is also an important magnet for tourism. Mount Fuji is also one of Japan's many UNESCO World Heritage Sites, and we have questioned what the purpose is of seeking this status. The chapter has also considered Japan's environmental issues, looking at how it has impacted the world around it, at times attempting to control it, and also how it has to respond to some of the natural challenges it faces. Due to the lack of natural resources, the need for alternative energy sources has been looked at, as well as how this relates to how Japan has had to respond to some of the impact of the Great East Japan Earthquake. Although the fact that the Kyōto Protocol was negotiated in Japan may mean that Japan has a special connection to environmental issues and taking an international lead, the scope would appear limited, as this chapter has also discussed how Japan continues some whaling in spite of international protests.

5

CORE VALUES

Japan is spiritual. In thinking about the symbols of Japan in Exercise 1.1, it may be that you included its Buddhist temples or Shintō shrines. Such places naturally become the focus for tourist activities in Japan. Consequently, it is natural to assume that most Japanese are religious. Yet many Japanese do not consider themselves to be religious. How can we explain this paradox? This is one of the questions that this chapter will address. As you will discover, central to much 'religious' activity in Japan are attitudes to death, and this chapter will look at how deaths are remembered and memorialised as an example of this. Building upon this, the chapter will then go on to consider another paradox: why is it that in a country where rituals relating to remembering and paying respects to the dead, in which celebrating the living is a key component, are so many seemingly prepared to end their own lives through suicide? The chapter concludes by looking at the ways in which religion may influence another part of Japanese society and culture: the nature of Japanese service. To help with our discussions about religion in Japan, please complete Exercise 5.1.

EXERCISE 5.1

Write down what the word 'religion' means to you. Think about how you would define this word and what are the key components of a religion.

RELIGION IN JAPAN

To help illustrate the complexity of understanding religion in Japan, let us begin by looking at some statistics. According to the survey done by the Agency for Cultural Affairs, the number of 'adherents' in 2011 was as follows: Shintō 100,771,000, Buddhism 84,708,000, Christianity 1,921,000, and other religions 9,490,000 (Ministry of Internal Affairs and Communications 2014). Consider what these figures show. The total comes to 196,891,000 – about 70 million more than the population of Japan. How could this be? Clearly, it reveals that Japanese people adhere to more than one religion. However, we need to be careful about using words such as 'adhere' or 'believe' in religion in relation to Japan. Buddhism and Shintō do not have equivalents of the Bible or Qur'an, and although there are stories relating to the creation of the world in Shintō that are no less scientific than those found in Genesis in the Bible, it may be that most registered Shintō 'adherers' do not give this aspect of the religion much credence. In Buddhism and Shintō, there is no need to pray each day or to attend a special venue on a particular day of the week, but the religions contain philosophies and practices that seemingly overlap with those that many Japanese hold, and there are particular acts that will be done at particular times. Consequently, part of the problem in trying to understand Japanese religions may be semantic. What 'religion' means to Japanese and non-Japanese may not be the same thing. The Japanese word for religion, *shūkyō*, was coined in the Meiji period and was created partly in relation to Japan's increased interactions with Christian countries (Isomae 2013). Questioning a Japanese person about 'religion' or '*shūkyō*' may lead to a response based upon a perception of what the word means to a non-Japanese rather than what it means to him or her.

Let us look at some practices relating to religion in Japan, as it is practice rather than belief that appears to be the defining feature of religion in Japan. Many practices relate to events in a person's life. Looking at these practices, you will see how there is a gradual shift from the significance of Shintō to Buddhism, although both may feature on any given day throughout their life (Hood 2012). But there is one area where Shintō and Buddhism are distinct, and that is their relationship to death. For Shintō, death is 'dirty' and something that should be avoided, and there are a number of purification rituals and practices to avoid connections to death. Buddhism, on the other hand, is the religion to which most Japanese will turn to for funerals and other death rituals. However, many Japanese will have a place to worship their ancestors in the home, and this practice unites Shintō and Buddhism. However, these ancestors are nameless and are only ever referred to as *senzo* ('the ancestors'), and the individual identities of former family members become merged into this collective 33 or 50 years after their death, depending on the Buddhist sect (Hood 2011: 115). Ancestor worship is said to have a long history in Japan, and many of the Kofun tombs are graphic symbols of this (see Chapter 6).

Central to Shintō is the idea of *kami* (deity). Anything potentially can be a *kami* – from natural phenomena to people, including historically the emperor. Traditionally each family had its own *kami*, and when families merged, through marriage for example, the resulting family would worship both *kami*. Consequently, the idea of polytheism has a rich history in Japan and is a reason why, for most Japanese, there is no issue adhering to both Shintō and Buddhist, or even to also be Christian despite its ideas of monotheism. Over time, events conspired to give some Japanese the belief that *kami* were protecting the nation as a whole. When two Mongol attacks against an almost defenceless Japan were seemingly thwarted by winds (*kaze*), a belief that these winds were sent by the *kami* developed, and so the word *kamikaze* was born. In the face of almost certain defeat towards the end of World War Two, the word took a new connotation, as is discussed below. In contemporary Japan, Shintō can still be seen being practised in a number of settings – from ceremonies marking the start of construction work, to prayers when constructing tunnels so as not to offend the *kami* of the mountain (Hood 2006a: 181–2), to prayers for the safe launch of a space rocket (Japan Today, 26 February 2014).

It is perhaps the lack of strong beliefs within Shintō and Buddhism that is why Japan has seen the creation of many 'new religions'. Of course, there are likely to be many who are 'adherers' to new religions who are also registered Buddhists, for example, or conduct various Shintō practices. Just as there are many sects within Buddhism, so there are many new religions. Most of the new religions take elements from other religions, while also bringing in additional teachings. It is not uncommon for these new religions to have a charismatic leader to help galvanise followers. Sōka Gakkai is one the largest of the new religions, and is significant due to its links with the political party New Komeitō, which is somewhat problematic due to the separation of politics and religion as set out in the Constitution. However, the most notorious is Aleph, or Aum Shinrikyō as it was formerly known and was called at the time of its attack on the Tōkyō metro system in 1995. But it is important to stress that most new religions do not appear to cause any problems, although non-Japanese media does have a tendency to focus on the 'stranger' practices of some seemingly without noting the similarity with more widely practised religions in some cases.

THE OSUTAKA PILGRIMAGE

Aiding a deceased love one to become one of the ancestors, as well as the need not to upset the ancestors, is an important driving force behind some of the religious practices that can be seen in Japan. To understand this, let us look at the example of the memorialisation of the victims of the world's largest single plane crash, which happened in Japan on 12 August 1985. The plane, a Boeing 747 specially adapted to carry additional passengers due to the demands of domestic transportation (see Chapter 3), was carrying a total of 524 crew and passengers and was on a flight from Haneda Airport to Itami Airport in Ōsaka. The plane crashed at 18:56 in the mountains of Ueno-mura. By the time the search and rescue teams arrived, just four survivors were found and 520 had perished. Every year, a variety of events take place around the anniversary of the crash to remember those who died. These are covered extensively by the Japanese media. Many will also travel to the village and crash site at other times of the year also, but here I will focus on the events around the anniversary, which I refer to as the 'Osutaka Pilgrimage'. There are three elements to the Osutaka Pilgrimage, and we will now look at each of these in the order in which they take place. As we do this, you should be thinking about the degree to which they could be considered religious.

Pilgrimage itself has a long history in Japan. For much of the Tokugawa period (1603–1868), travel from one part of Japan to another was largely prohibited other than for religious reasons. As a consequence, pilgrimages that combined both a religious and a ludic element developed as a means for people to travel for pleasure (Hood 2011: 21). Perhaps the most well-known pilgrimage is that of the 88 temples and shrines of Shikoku, as discussed in detail by Reader (1993). However, there are many other pilgrimages such as the Saikoku in the Kansai region of Japan. What is noticeable about all of these is that they involve visiting more than one location. If we do not restrict ourselves to thinking that pilgrimages have to have a religious element, it is possible to see that visits to tourist spots such as Tōkyō Disneyland, Tōkyō Sky Tree and Tōkyō Tower as part of a school trip or a visit to the capital could also be seen as a form of pilgrimage.

The first part of the Osutaka Pilgrimage takes place on 11 August, when the bereaved hold a service, known as *tōrōnagashi*, where messages are written on lanterns, inside which are candles that are lit, and the lanterns are floated down the river in Ueno-mura (see Figure 5.1). This is reminiscent to what is done in some other areas to mark the Obon festival and also in Hiroshima on the anniversary of the atomic bombing. As well as speeches, a minute's silence and songs, bubbles are released at the end of the event. The fact that the crash happened on 12 August, which is seen as the start of Obon in many parts of Japan, probably adds extra poignancy for some. Obon may be translated into English as the 'festival of the dead', and is considered to be a time when the spirits of dead relatives come down from the mountains to their ancestral village (Tamaru and Reid 1996: 81). But how many participating in the *tōrōnagashi* actually believe that their messages on the lanterns will be read by the spirits of their loved ones? Here, we can perhaps draw parallels with the discussion in Chapter 1 about British people and events on 5 November, for example.

Many Japanese will travel to see relatives at Obon, taking time to go to the ancestral grave and clean it. However, it is important to stress that Obon tends to be a cheerful event with dancing and the focus is on the celebration of life, and so death memorialisation is rarely morbid or ghoulish. Obon is a time when many companies will allow employees to take holiday, regardless of whether they are taking part in any of the activities normally associated with the festival or not. Consequently, trains and planes tend to be full at the start and end of Obon and long tailbacks on the expressways are also common.

The second part of the Osutaka Pilgrimage takes place on 12 August, when a memorial service is held at the crash site. The

Figure 5.1 The Osutaka Pilgrimage. Top left: The focal point of the crash site on Osutaka-no-One. Top right: the memorial post for Hisashi Ōshima (a.k.a. Kyū Sakamoto). Bottom left: the tōrōnagashi. Bottom right: memorial service at Irei-no-Sono.

crash site today is known as Osutaka-no-One, literally 'the ridge on Osutaka', a name that reflects the popular understanding of the name of the mountain on which the plane crashed. In fact, the plane came down on a ridge on Mount Takamagahara, but by the time this was known many elements of the media had reported the site to be on Mount Osutaka, and this is the name that stuck. The focal point of the site today is located where a heliport was made following the crash. Around this area, there are memorial stones, a bell, places for people to write messages and a statue of Kannon, the Bodhisattva of Mercy. A memorial service is held in the morning, including speeches, a minute's silence, songs and the blowing of bubbles.

After remains were identified, marker posts were placed in the appropriate area at the crash site. Many families have subsequently placed their own memorial posts there, which may be replaced from time to time. The design of the marker posts can vary quite significantly. Many of the posts are wooden, while there are many stone ones and also metal memorials. The way in which the name is written on the post can also vary. Some will use the person's Buddhist posthumous name, but many more have the person's actual name. There are also many examples of where a message rather than a name is written.

Many families who visit the crash site continue to place a range of items at the site by the marker posts. These items can include toys (as for the families their loved one never grows up, but is frozen in time), flowers, food and drink. Some posts also have photos of the victim, while other photos, both recent and those including the victim, may be placed by the marker post. Next to some, and at the main memorial stone, are *sotoba* posts with Buddhist phrases written on them. New *sotoba* may be placed at memorial stones each year, with the others left to rot naturally. As well as the *sotoba*, a number of crucifixes can be found for both Japanese and non-Japanese victims.

The third part of the Osutaka Pilgrimage takes place in the evening of 12 August, when two back-to-back ceremonies are held at Irei-no-Sono back in the centre of the village (see Figure 5.1). The first of these sees families, people from the village, JAL and others place flowers in front of the memorial tower. There are also a number of short speeches and a minute's silence. In the second ceremony, families light 520 candles to remember the victims. A minute's silence is then held to coincide with the time of the crash.

The memorialisation relating to the JL123 crash has become about more than simply this crash itself, as other tragedies are also remembered. Representatives of associations connected to these accidents are often also present at the ceremonies, and so JL123 may be influencing how other tragedies are remembered, as well as reflecting aspects of memorialisation that are commonly found in Japan. That the media follows the Osutaka Pilgrimage ensures that the crash will never be forgotten and indeed will be introducing it to a generation born after the crash happened. This process, together with films, dramas and documentaries relating to the crash that continue to be produced, are probably fuelling interest in the crash. In this respect, JL123 is arguably the Japanese equivalent of the story of the sinking of the *Titanic*.

Looking at the memorialisation JL123 may lead you to believe that much effort is put into remembering the dead in Japan. Anniversaries, such as those for the bombings of Hiroshima and Nagasaki, appear to be particularly pertinent when the deaths were 'untimely'. But there is a place in Japan that has become synonymous with suicides, and this seems to be the antithesis of the activities in Ueno-mura.

AOKIGAHARA

While suicide is a national issue, it is one forest, Aokigahara Jukai, that has become most associated with suicide in Japan. If you do a quick search on the Internet you will likely find many pages referring to Aokigahara as being Japan's number one suicide spot, and it is apparently second only to the Golden Gate Bridge globally. You may also read that compasses do not work in Aokigahara, due either to the volcanic rocks or 'the evils' in the area, and that even GPS does not work. Why is there such interest in Aokigahara? Why do Japanese people go there to commit suicide? These are two of the questions that this section will address through my own visit to the forest and research about what goes on there. The implications, however, are much broader than what takes place in Aokigahara alone.

The forest itself is at the north-western foot of Mount Fuji and is located on a lava flow resulting from an eruption in 864 that separated a lake there into three parts. The forest itself is about 3,000 hectares (Yamanashi Tourism Organisation 2014). In other words, it is about half the size of the land inside the Yamanote Line in Tōkyō, although some websites suggest it is about the same size. The forest is split into two main sections due to the roads that run through it: a larger southern section and a smaller northern section. The two sections are quite different, and we will look at both of them in turn. For note, at no point did I have any problems with my compass or GPS signal. I even got a better mobile phone signal than I often get in cities in Japan.

In the southern section, one can find a wide and well-developed path that forms part of the Tōkai Nature Trail, which stretches from Tōkyō to Ōsaka. Within this part of Aokigahara, you can find the Wind Cave and Ice Cave. You will also find the sign proclaiming that we are in Aokigahara Jukai (see Figure 5.2). This is the sign that seems to feature in all books, articles, TV documentaries and films that feature Aokigahara. The sign points out that the area is rich with nature. Although it may be hard to see much wildlife, there is much other life. The area is damp and it is relatively bright, which makes excellent conditions for moss and lichen to grow across the exposed roots of trees and across rocks. That there is so much vegetation around makes it easy to see that there are no signs of people having left the main path to go deeper into the forest. Even when there are tracks going into the forest, it would appear from the lack of footprints, for example, that people are observing the basic no entry signs and ropes. At the end of the trail near the Ice Cave, there is a sign calling upon people to think about the importance of life, and to think about their parents, siblings and children, adding that one-to-one consultation is possible by calling a particular number. When I visited the Ice Cave, there was also a poster there with information about a missing person from Hiroshima. Back in the forest, the only evidence I saw of Aokigahara's more notorious side was of some flowers resting on a moss-covered rock. Was this left where somebody had committed suicide or just at a convenient location? It was the first, and indeed only, sign I saw of any memorialisation akin to that I had seen many times at Osutaka-no-One.

The small northern section is very different to the southern section, and is even quite hard to access, with no obvious entrance

Figure 5.2 Aokigahara. Top left: the lava spill on which Aokigahara has grown can be seen coming down to Lake Saiko with Mount Fuji in the background. Top right: the sign for Aokigahara Jukai. Middle left: a sign calling upon those considering suicide to think of their family first. Middle: a rope with signs saying no entrance and that there is CCTV (despite no visible signs of any, or even electricity) block a track into the woods. Middle right: a sign providing details of a help number for those with financial problems. Bottom left: flowers left on a moss-covered rock. Bottom middle: drink cans and empty packets of pills. Bottom right: do a blue sheet and bags mark the spot where somebody tried to commit suicide?

to it. As soon as you enter, there is both a sign calling on those considering committing suicide to think of their families and friends and another nearby with details about what number to call if the person has financial problems. Loan sharks and associated issues are a major problem in Japan. In this section of the forest, there are many smaller paths. There are no signs saying no entry. Soon after entering the northern section, I started seeing tape, which may be used for cordoning off a section. Then I came across items that may be testament to Aokigahara's notoriety: empty bottles, cans of alcohol and packets of pills. Was this the scene where somebody overdosed to kill him or herself? Or signs of a failed attempt? At another site, there were blue sheets left behind. Were these sheets used by the person him or herself as he or she prepared him or herself or by those who came later to cover the body? But why would there be so many things left behind? Not clearing it away could present a signal that this is the 'right area' for committing suicide. With regular patrols by the police and local volunteers trying to clear away bodies or prevent others committing suicide, it seems odd more is not done to clear the forest. After all, there has even been consideration of having a large wall being put round Aokigahara to stop people from entering. Yamanashi prefecture has also now banned TV camera crews from filming in the forest in an attempt to reduce the public awareness of the site (News on Japan, 6 September 2013).

If we look at where suicides take place in Japan, we find that in 2009, for example, the municipality that had the highest number was Adachi ward in Tōkyō, with 167 suicides (Cabinet Office 2010). Another 25 municipalities had at least 100 suicides, and 13 of the 23 wards of Tōkyō had at least 71 suicides. The 78th on the list is the town of Fuji-Kawaguchi-ko. It is this town and the neighbouring township where Aokigahara lies. But while Kawaguchi-ko-machi may be low on the list, compared to many of those higher up the list there is a smaller variation in identifiable locations within it. Another significant point about the suicides in Kawaguchi-ko-machi is that the majority of suicides are by people from outside the town. For most municipalities, there is not a great difference between where the person was from and where they committed suicide. But in 2009, for example, there were 42 municipalities where there were at least 10 less bodies recovered there than the number of people from that municipality that committed suicide. In other words, people from these places had gone from their home area to somewhere else to commit suicide. While most of these 42 municipalities were close to 10, Nerima ward in Tōkyō had the greatest difference with 31. So where are people going to commit suicide? In many cases, it would appear that they are committing suicide in another ward within the same city, for example. This may be where the suicide takes place at work, for example. For smaller cities, this would explain why there is little difference between the reported suicides and the number of people from that municipality who committed suicide. For larger cities, it would explain why we may see Nerima at the top of this chart, while other Tōkyō wards are net importers of suicides.

Whereas movement within cities and suicides at workplaces may account for many of the geographical shifts, it clearly does not explain them all. What is notable from a list of 31 municipalities where the number of suicides was at least 10 greater than the number of people from that area who had committed suicide is the number of municipalities that stand out as areas that contain parks and other tourist spots. High up this list are both Kawaguchi-ko-machi, which is the highest net importer with 65, and the neighbouring township of Narusawa, where none of the 19 suicides was by locals. Many of these would have been in Aokigahara. We need to remember that these figures only account for those cases where bodies have been found, and in the case of Aokigahara this may not always happen. The figures also overlook the number of failed attempts.

So while Aokigahara is certainly noteworthy in terms of it being a net importer of suicides, it does not tell us why people go there to commit suicide. After all, it is not even an easy place to get to. If starting from Tōkyō, for example, and taking public transport, a combination of trains and a bus will be needed and it will take around three hours, assuming that the connections have been favourable. If going by car, it may be possible to get to Aokigahara in about two hours. As suggested earlier, people may even be travelling to Aokigahara from much further afield. There are many other places that people could stop off en route, so why Aokigahara? Aokigahara's notoriety seems to have started with the novel *Nami no Tō* by Seichō Matsumoto, in which two lovers commit suicide in the forest at the end of the story. It was also turned into a film in 1960, and there have been no less than seven TV dramatisations. It also features in the million-selling book *Kanzen Jisatsu Manyuaru* (*Complete Manual of Suicide*), published in 1993. Although one has to wonder whether such a book is really what somebody considering suicide turns to, it does include six pages about how to get to Aokigahara, where to go and things to be aware of. Perhaps significantly, the book also contains a map of Aokigahara that includes three suggested areas for where to commit suicide in the forest, with the northern section being one of them and the location where I found the flowers being another.

There can be no doubt that Aokigahara has become associated with suicides. While it may not be surprising to find an article about it in a Japan-based newspaper, such as the English-language newspaper *The Japan Times*, which ran a feature article on 26 June 2011, it also features in articles in newspapers from around the world. For example, you can find two articles in the British newspaper *The Daily Telegraph* in different years (5 November 2000 and 4 May 2009). There is also no shortage of websites, although many of these tend to replicate limited information, often relying on a few other websites for pictures and regurgitation of unreferenced facts and data, and making out that Aokigahara is 'scary' or 'haunted'.

While there are many articles in English-language papers around the world and in Japan, there appear to be less in the Japanese newspapers. It is almost as though what goes on there is being ignored. More significantly, it may be that Japan is ignoring the root causes of the suicides. Why would this be? Perhaps we can find the answer through looking at why there may be international interest in Aokigahara. Japan is a country that is often associated with suicide, thanks in part to its history of *seppuku* and the *tokubetsu kōgekitai*, more commonly known as *kamikaze*. Consequently, perhaps suicide is discussed in relation to Japan more than some of the other countries where it is even more prevalent. Do some go looking for these stories that satisfy the cliché?

Figure 5.3 shows the number of suicides and the suicide rate in Japan each year from 1899 to 2012. You can see from this figure that the number of suicides has risen in recent times, and was above 30,000 per year for a number of years. This means that the number that commit suicide each year in Japan was nearly double the number that died in the 2011 Great East Japan Earthquake (Cabinet Office 2014). You can also see that the suicide rate has been comparable to the levels in the 1950s, but for much of the intervening 30 years it was as low as half that rate. In terms of doing research, this highlights an important lesson: the need to check data for yourself. When I was conducting research about education in Japan, I came across sources – which I will not name to save any embarrassment for the authors – that referred to the relatively high suicide rate in Japan. But rather than using the raw data, the sources were referring to other academic texts. Following this chain of references, I found that they were ultimately referring to data from the 1950s, and so were some 30 years out of date.

Although the suicide rate has varied over time, it is relatively high compared to many nations around the world, and is about double the OECD average (OECD 2014). Is the high rate because many Japanese consider suicide to be 'honourable'? I have come across many Japanese who do not hold such a view. Perhaps what is of greater significance is that there is no overwhelming condemnation of suicide in Japan, as may exist in some other cultures. In other words, while Japanese society does not actively support or condone suicide, perhaps not enough is done to stop it. The Japanese government has even been slow to act upon the problem of loan sharks, which are often seen as being one of the

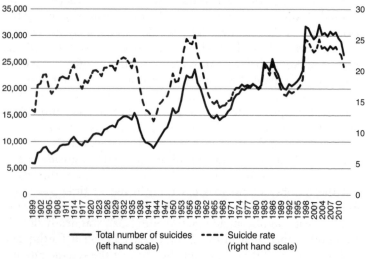

Figure 5.3 Suicides in Japan, 1899–2012

Source: Figure by the author based on data from Nenji-toukei (2014b).

elements that drive many to suicide. With financial problems being a major factor in why some commit suicide, why has the Japanese government been so slow to introduce legislation limiting the amounts of interest loan sharks could charge? Do those who offer such loans have some sort of influence within government?

Each year, the Japanese Kanji Proficiency Society chooses a particular *kanji* that best reflects the mood of the year that has just ended. The *kanji* for 2011 was *kizuna* (絆), which can be translated as bonds. This *kanji* was chosen in part as it reflected the response to the Great East Japan Earthquake and the way in which people revealed the importance of the bonds between not only the living, but also between the living and those who lost their lives as a result of the disaster. Osutaka-no-One and the Osutaka Pilgrimage is all about *kizuna*. It provides many insights into certain norms in relation to memorialisation practices associated to the *kizuna* between the living and the dead, and between the living and the living. On the other hand, Aokigahara is a place where those who reject such practices go to die. Aokigahara may be the exception that proves the rule about the importance of memorialisation and *kizuna*, for the key issue is that Aokigahara, more than many other suicide spots in Japan, goes totally against what we have seen in relation to the Osutaka Pilgrimage, for example. Those who go to Aokigahara to commit suicide are going out of their way to potentially not be discovered. People may not know when they died. The memorials that are conducted on specific days after a death cannot be performed. It may be that even the correct year may not be known depending on when the body is found, if it is ever found. It will be hard for them to become an ancestor.

While statistically the number of suicides in Aokigahara is not high in relation to the number of suicides that take place in Japan each year, it has seemingly become the means by which those outside of Japan can frame the discussion of suicide within Japan. But do such stories tell us more about Japan or those looking at Japan? What are the consequences of such stories? By highlighting the lengths to which some go to commit suicide in Japan, does it further nurture the idea that the Japanese as a whole are somehow different? Is there an underlying idea that 'different' means 'strange' or 'odd'? Why do we not read more about the

Golden Gate Bridge being the world's number one suicide spot? Why are the patrols of people on the lookout for people who may be about to commit suicide in Aokigahara more newsworthy than those at Beachy Head in the UK, for example? Why would a photograph of the sign asking for people to think of their family before committing suicide in Aokigahara be of more interest than the one suggesting that someone call the Samaritans before leaping from the Clifton Suspension Bridge in the UK? That stories in the non-Japanese media about Japan present Japan in a certain light to reinforce stereotypes or to detract from issues and problems that may be just as prevalent in the reader's own country is an issue that we have touched upon before, and is one of the issues that you should be most aware of as you continue your studies of Japan.

Other than the suicides in Aokigahara, the other well-known aspects of suicide in Japan tend to be the historical aspects of *hara-kiri* by *samurai* and the *kamikaze* pilots of the Second World War. The planes that the pilots flew were called *Ōka*, which means cherry blossom. Cherry blossom is also linked to the deaths of *samurai*; life may be beautiful, but short (Ollhoff 2010: 12). There is a strong connection between death and cherry blossom, which is more commonly known as *sakura*. The twentieth-century writer Motojirō Kajii (1924) wrote, 'Dead bodies are buried under the cherry trees', and suggested that these bodies were the reason for the blossom's beauty. Many Japanese will say that their appreciation of the beauty of cherry blossom is derived from the intrinsic appeal of *mono-no-aware*, the transience of things; the cherry blossom is at its most beautiful as it falls from the tree and dies. But if this is really the case, why is it that during *hanami*, when Japanese will flock to parks to drink beneath the trees, so few are concerned with any falling blossom, let alone continuing the tradition of writing any poetry while they are there? If the falling of the cherry blossom is so significant, why are there so few photographs taken of it? While capturing a single flower falling would require patience and a degree of luck, as well as skill, the same can be said for many photographs. Surely there should be more evidence to support the idea that Japanese people actually believe the blossoms are at their most beautiful as they fall from the tree. But cherry blossom are not only associated with death. The blooming of the cherry blossom is also often associated with the start of the academic year, although due to the nature of seasons in Japan (as discussed in Chapter 4) the image applies to only select parts of the country. The sight of cherry blossom is a major tourist draw, particularly for certain cities that have become noted for the beauty of their trees.

This chapter has suggested that for most Japanese, there is an acceptance of death as a part of a life cycle, and that even the beauty of *sakura* may be derived from dead bodies. However, there is another side to death in Japan. As pointed out earlier, for Shintō, death is considered to be 'dirty' and something that should be avoided. More than this, those connected with death itself should also be avoided. This led to the development of discrimination against those who were regularly connected with death, such as undertakers and those involved in the killing of animals and making leather from their skins, for example. While officially this class of '*eta*' was abolished in the Meiji period, those who still work in these areas, as well as those related to the former *eta*, still face discrimination today. The *burakumin*, as they are referred to in contemporary Japan, may be ethnically Japanese, but they will often find it hard to gain acceptance in mainstream Japanese society. This can lead to problems with finding marriage partners and getting employment outside of work associated with *burakumin*. Why has the government seemingly done so little to address the problems that the *burakumin* face? You should keep the issues that the *burakumin* face in mind when we discuss issues relating to group harmony, for example, in Chapter 7.

OMOTENASHI

So where do we draw the line with religion in Japan? We have already seen that much of the basis of 'religion' in Japan is about practice rather than belief. This allows for the coexistence of Shintō and Buddhism, which are further underpinned by some Confucian values. We can see a range of examples of behaviour that appear to be drawn from ideas of purity, which may come from Shintō. For example, that Japanese people will remove their shoes on entering a house and put on slippers is said to aid with keeping the house clean, preserving the inside from outside impurities. And yet they will wear the same clothes and not necessarily wash their hands upon entering the house. I have come across many Japanese who have other reasons for removing their shoes than 'purity' reasons, with comfort being the most given.

Another area where we can apparently see the desire to maintain purity is with the wearing of white gloves by train drivers (see Figure 5.4) and taxi drivers, for example. But perhaps it is more beneficial to focus not so much on whether there are quasi-religious reasons for gloves being worn, but more how they are seen by the people using them as just part of a sign of high-quality service. The word to describe this ethos in Japanese is *omotenashi*, which can be translated as hospitality, entertainment or service. None cover the nuance that the word has in Japanese, and so apparently the Japanese word has been 'introduced into the

Figure 5.4 Omotenashi. A *shinkansen* driver points to acknowledge the change in speed limit as it approaches a station stop. Note also the space in the dashboard for the traditional pocket watch.

glossary of the hospitality industry' (Horisaka 2013). Indeed, much of what we have discussed in Chapter 3 about the high-quality service provided on the *shinkansen* and the training that is required relates to *omotenashi*.

Although Horisaka suggests that it was the 1964 Tōkyō Olympics that introduced *omotenashi* to the world, I would suggest that it has not become widely known to date. Perhaps the Tōkyō 2020 Olympics will have more success in that regard – particularly if books such as this one keep mentioning it, so that more visitors to Japan become familiar with concept and actively go looking for examples of it. Yet although the concept has existed in Japan for many years and the word itself has been used in Japan for a long time, the word has seemingly become used more prevalently in recent years. The concept was encapsulated in the 2013 movie *Kenchō Omotenashi Ka* (Yoshishige Miyake, 2013) (*Hospitality Department*), which was based on the 2011 novel of the same name by Hiro Arikawa, and centres on the attempts to introduce the concept of *omotenashi* to a department in spirit rather than just the name. The word was even included in the candidature speech for the Tōkyō 2020 Olympic bid given by Prime Minister Abe in Buenos Aires in 2013. In 2014, when JR East announced that it would be introducing a new luxury tourist *shinkansen* complete with foot spas and *tatami* seating areas, it was reported as being a form of *omotenashi* when announced to the media (e.g. *The Japan Times*, 5 March 2014), even though it was not mentioned in the official press release (JR East 2014).

So what is *omotenashi*? According to Muneyuki Jōraku, who has done research about *omotenashi* culture and is involved in the marketing section of a Japanese hotel chain, the key components are that 'the host anticipates the needs of the guest in advance and offers a pleasant service that guests do not expect', but provides the hospitality without any hierarchical relationship between the server and customer (Wattention 2014). That the customer is also considered a *kami-sama* (deity) rather than merely a king in Japan would suggest that there is still some form of hierarchical thinking in relation to service even in Japan. Jōraku points out that anticipating a guest's needs may be particularly important in Japan, as guests have a tendency not to make direct requests as this would be 'considered unsophisticated in Japan'. If part of *omotenashi* is to provide service that guests do not expect, surely this leads to expectations about what future service should be? Clearly, the concept is hard to explain and pin down, but on the whole you know it when you see it, even if at times there may be a feeling that it leads to excesses. This may be particularly the case if you come from a background of striving for efficiency (see Chapter 6).

But does all this mean that *omotenashi* is natural and cannot be trained? Is it something that is inherently Japanese? I would suggest that although there are numerous examples of good service in Japan, it is far from universal, which would suggest that elements have to be trained into staff also. However, such training itself may undo some of the *omotenashi*. For example, when asking people about the differences between service on ANA and JAL, many have commented on how stewardesses appear to smile on ANA because they want to, whereas on JAL they would appear to smile as they have been told to do so in a particular situation. Whether it is really possible to make such a distinction even after using both airlines many times is perhaps something that you should also test when you use different companies.

The existence of *omotenashi* can even be seen in how global brands may operate differently in Japan to some other countries. A visit to McDonald's in Japan will reveal that the final item on the menu is a 'Smile', which will cost you ¥0. Do staff at McDonald's Japan smile more than their counterparts in other countries? Is the item on the menu a reminder to the customer that they should be receiving a smile or to the staff that they should be providing one? If smiling is such an inherent part of *omotenashi*, why is there a need for the item on the menu at all? Surely something that is naturally a part of Japanese service, or at least part of the service that staff are trained to provide, would not require any form of reminder. The smile is not the only item on the menu that may be unfamiliar to foreign visitors to McDonald's Japan. Whether the other food items can be seen as a further example of *omotenashi* or whether it is merely good business sense to provide items that are likely to be more popular with local diners than the standard McDonald's menu is something I will leave you to consider.

SUMMARY

In this chapter, we have discussed a range of issues that have, in some form, a connection with religion and the practices of Japanese people. Indeed, we have seen that in studying Japan, practice rather than belief is what is central to religion in Japan, and so drawing a line between religion, philosophy and normal behaviour becomes very difficult. It also means that when watching seemingly religious behaviour, such as the memorial events as part of a pilgrimage, one cannot be sure about the degree to which the practices are being conducted due to belief in what underpins them rather than due to tradition and expectation. The chapter went on to suggest that some of these beliefs have come to be reflected in the way in which service is provided in Japan in the form of *omotenashi*, which may also reflect other aspects of Japanese culture and the Japanese language.

6

PURE JAPANESE

Japan is nationalistic. While the previous chapter discussed the openness of religion in Japan and how the focus on practice appears to allow Japanese people to be very accepting of a number of different religions to be pursued at the same time, the existence of nationalism would appear to suggest that most Japanese are more closed and insular in their beliefs about Japan's position in the world. Potent symbols such as the emperor, visits to the controversial Yasukuni Shrine by politicians, and the usage of the national flag, *Hinomaru*, and national anthem, *Kimigayo*, at a range of events appear to be symbolic of this nationalism. However, while non-Japanese media in particular seem to be fond of espousing the idea that nationalism is on the rise in Japan, what is the basis for such stories? In what ways is this nationalism different to what may be found in the countries whose media print such stories? How does nationalism relate to Japan's territorial disputes and discussions about the role of Japan's military forces today? How is nationalism also a force within the actions of Japanese consumers and businesses?

Before we begin to look at the issues to be covered in this chapter, please complete Exercise 6.1.

Nationalism assumes the existence of a nation. It would also further imply the existence of other nations, for otherwise there

EXERCISE 6.1

Answer the following questions:

- What is your race?
- What is your ethnicity?
- What is your nationality?
- What is your blood group?
- Do you believe it is necessary to speak the national language to hold the passport of a nation?
- How often were the national flag or anthem used at your school?
- How important is where you are educated central to your national identity?

would be little need to define one's own nation. This means that nationalism would appear to have the need to highlight difference as its heart. This is divergent in its nature. But nationalism means different things to different people. It is a problematic word, as it appears to cover a wide range of concepts and can be viewed as a positive trait by some, but a dangerous force by others. The debate over nationalism has suffered from oversimplification, generalisations and misunderstandings about terms, ideas and truths. Perhaps due to Japan's actions in relation to the Second World War, with its involvement in that conflict associated with nationalism, there is a tendency for discussions in English about Japanese nationalism to assume that it is something to be wary of. However, as we shall see throughout this chapter, the scope of nationalism means that there are situations where actions could be described as nationalistic, but many Japanese would not see it as being negative. But where do we draw the line between nationalism and patriotism, a word that rarely carries any negative connotations, for example? Why is it that we will find few references to Japanese behaving patriotically in the non-Japanese media? Why is it that we may even find use of the word ultra-nationalistic, with its apparent negative image, in relation to Japanese politicians when politicians with similar ideologies and behaviour in other countries will not have such a label attached to them?

When it comes to understanding issues related to nationalism in Japan, it is often in relation to a person's view on issues relating to Japan's role in the Second World War that can be instructive. In this respect, you may find it helpful to read *Japan's Contested War Memories* (Seaton 2007). At the same time, keep in mind that just as there are a variety of different words in English, so there are in Japanese too, each with their own nuances. Rather than dwell too much on definitions, what is central to our study here is how forms of nationalism are played out in Japanese society.

WHO ARE THE JAPANESE?

Part of the problem of nationalism can be how it relates to ethnicity, race and even definitions about the geographic boundaries of the nation. In other words, what does it mean to be a Japanese person and where is Japan? Let us initially consider the first of these questions. Throughout the book, we have been discussing 'the Japanese', but what do we actually mean by this? The answer to this highlights a number of complex interrelated issues. To help us deal with this, let us consider a number of questions and their answers.

First of all, is there a Japanese race? While someone acting against Japanese people may be termed a 'racist', which would appear to suggest that there is a Japanese race, such a convention reflects a looseness with how we use terms and our understanding of them rather than the existence of the race itself. Anthropologists generally point to there being three main races: Negroid, Mongoloid and Caucasoid (e.g. Yoshino 1995: 22). Of course, many people are a combination of these races. In fact, when most speak of 'race', what they actually mean is 'ethnicity'. But even the concept of ethnicity is not without its complications. While some Japanese will refer to the Japanese as being 'pure', a study of most Japanese people's DNA is likely to reveal the influence of at least one other ethnic group. Much of this influence has come from back in history. While it is thought that there were people on the islands of Japan going back at least 30,000 years, these people may have been wiped out or assimilated by people coming from the Asian continent during the Yayoi period

(300 BC–AD 300). But since this influence is from nearly 2,000 years ago, should we consider the overwhelming majority of the Japanese population as homogeneous and 'pure' ethnically Japanese?

The significance of having Japanese blood can also be seen in the fact that being born in Japan does not guarantee access to a Japanese passport (i.e. Japanese nationality). Indeed, there are many who have been born in Japan who have been largely regarded as foreigners and have had some of their rights limited as a result. The largest number of these people are those whose ethnic background is predominantly Korean or Chinese. Despite the fact that they may have been born in Japan, been educated in Japan, speak Japanese and may even have a Japanese name, the system has not regarded them as Japanese (for further discussion about this, see Weiner 2009). On the other hand, there have been other groups of people who have been born in another country, have not received a Japanese education and do not speak Japanese who have found it easier to get Japanese citizenship. The difference is their ethnicity. These people, known as *Nikkeijin*, are the descendants of Japanese immigrants to countries in South America in the 1930s in particular.

The relatively favourable treatment of *Nikkeijin*, at least in terms of being able to gain citizenship in Japan, speaks to the significance of ethnicity and blood in discussions about Japanese identity. Indeed, some Japanese pay particular attention to the blood group of potential partners when considering their characteristics. The importance of lineage can also be seen in relation to issues of imperial succession. The emperor remains a key symbol of Japan, and the years, at least on official documents, are generally counted using a system based on the imperial reign, as discussed in Chapter 1. Some Japanese claim that the ancestry of the current emperor can be traced back through an unbroken line to the first emperor, Jimmu, a direct descendent of the sun deity, Amaterasu. Although there is some debate about background of some of the early emperors, their significance cannot be ignored and the apparent burial mound for another early emperor, Nintoku (reigned 313–399), is one of the largest monuments in Japan (see Figure 6.1).

Figure 6.1 Daisen Kofun. This burial mound (*kofun*) is apparently for Emperor Nintoku and measures some 486 long and 305 wide, with the highest point being 35 metres. Despite its area being nearly three times the size of the base of the Great Pyramid of Giza, this and other *kofun* are not well-known outside of Japan.

While *Nikkeijin* may be able to get Japanese citizenship, that does not mean that they have not faced other challenges. But these have not been as a result of race, ethnicity or nationality, but due to 'culture'. With their upbringing in South America, the *Nikkeijin* who move to Japan will not only speak a different first language, but also have a different cultural behaviour. These differences have led to a variety of tensions. But they have not been the only group that has faced such tensions. Another group where possible cultural differences have been an area of concern has been the *kikokushijo*. These are children who spend an extended period living overseas before returning to Japan, often to re-enter the education system. But rather than fully embrace their international experience, Japan has seemingly been more concerned about their lack of exposure to the Japanese education system and developing the usual Japanese attributes, whatever they may be. So while some universities may have a quota for *kikokushijo* so that they may enter without requiring to undergo the usual examining faced by other Japanese students, the government has been keen to promote and develop Japanese schools overseas so that these children can receive at least some remedial Japanese education. Although in some cases this may amount to only one day (e.g. Saturday) of classes a week, the fact that such schools have been established would appear to speak to a larger concern about what the impact is of not having such knowledge or experience. For further information about *kikokushijo*, see *A Sociology of Japanese Youth* (Goodman *et al.* 2012).

That access to Japanese schooling is an issue points to why some have sought to make changes to the education system itself in order to foster greater patriotism in Japanese children. Prime Minister Nakasone started a programme of education reform in the 1980s that had this as a central component, and although many of the parts he may have wished to see altered did not happen during his tenure, the agenda was set and so it was not a surprise to see further changes consistent with his agenda being implemented in later years (Hood 2001). Perhaps the most controversial of these was the change to the Fundamental Law of Education (FLE) in 2006. The FLE is perhaps best understood as a Bill of Rights for education in Japan and was established by the Occupation following Japan's defeat in the Second World War, where the education system was seen as being central in fostering a nationalistic sentiment and devotion to the emperor. The key change to the FLE was the introduction of the concept of fostering an attitude to respect the traditions and culture of Japan and 'love the country and region that nurtured them' (MEXT 2006). The degree to which there have been any tangible differences in what Japanese schoolchildren believe or practise since the change to the FLE is something that you should explore further.

But it is worth stressing that even Nakasone saw what he called 'healthy' (*kenzen*) or 'justifiable' (*tadashii*) nationalism as a necessary component of internationalism. Perhaps it would be better to see this concept as 'healthy internationalism' (Hood 2001), which would reflect Nakasone's idea that:

> Each country has a long history, traditions and culture . . . its heritage. That is the foundation . . . It is to love the long history, traditions and culture. On top of this, it is then to use them to contribute to the rest of the world. Without knowing the foundation, you cannot exchange with other countries . . . It is to plant a flower of Japan in the global garden.
>
> (Nakasone interview, 15 March 2000)

Whether the children actually come to believe in these ideas is another matter. But as we have discussed in relation to religion, practice does not always require belief.

Nakasone's view perhaps does not fit with the comparative study of 'cultural nationalism' by Yoshino. Yoshino (1995: 109) concluded that while for British people an important aspect of being British are cultural things such as drinking tea, going to the pub and an appreciation of the British sense of humour, this was not the case for Japanese, with blood and ethnicity being more significant, as we have already discussed. Yet as Nakasone suggests, an appreciation of Japanese culture clearly is important at times, even if it is not a defining element of being Japanese. But what do we mean by culture in this context? More often than not, rather than including popular culture, it refers to 'high culture' such as *ikebana*, the Japanese tea ceremony, and such like. Women may go to lessons to learn how to do such things in order to add it to their profile for dating agencies when seeking potential marriage partners. Yet having the opportunities to use these skills in practice, particularly in the home after marriage, is likely to be limited. Why, then, would so many go out of their way to learn such 'traditional' cultural practices when there seems to be such limited interest in partaking in them?

Returning to the education system, this was also critical in relation to another nationalistic issue. Publicly funded schools are required to raise the national flag, *Hinomaru*, and play the national anthem, *Kimigayo*, at school graduation ceremonies and entrance ceremonies. However, this has long been opposed by many teachers and their unions, and so the actual usage varied greatly across the country. The issue came to a head in 1999 when teachers at one school stood their ground and refused to cooperate with the requirement, with part of the argument being that neither had official national status. Unable to broker an agreement, the principal of the school committed suicide. In an exceptionally short period of time, bills were passed through the Diet that formally established the national flag and anthem (Hood 2001: 64–8). Since then, official usage rates have seemingly been 100 per cent, but one has to question the accuracy of some of the statistics and whether both symbols are necessarily being used as one may expect (see Hood 2001: 68). Whether using these symbols actually leads to a development in patriotism or nationalism is another matter.

While the definitions of nationalism, patriotism and other similar concepts vary from country to country, there is one thing that we cannot escape. By creating a definition of what is necessary to be Japanese, say, opens the avenue to discrimination towards those who live in that country but do not have the required attributes. Even many *Nikkeijin* who seemingly possess the apparent key component of being Japanese have faced a variety of forms of discrimination. Given the discussions in Chapter 2 about the labour shortage Japan is facing, and taking into account what we have looked at in this chapter, to what degree do you think that mass immigration would be a practical solution? Of course, not all non-Japanese face discrimination, and some even have a degree of 'positive discrimination'. Furthermore, we must remember that even many 'pure' Japanese, such as the *burakumin* discussed in Chapter 5, can be subject to discrimination. The seeming homogeneity of the Japanese has led to the development of the idea of uniqueness. This is the essence of a body of literature known as *Nihonjinron*, which has been used to help 'explain' a variety of differences in Japanese cultural behaviour.

It is not uncommon to find articles in foreign media suggesting that nationalism is rising in Japan. Such articles have been being printed for many years, if not decades. What is generally lacking in such articles is evidence to support this. Surely after all of these years, we should be able to find clear signs of this increased nationalism, which, as pointed out earlier, is, at implied level at least, somehow different and more dangerous than the patriotism that would be found in that country of the foreign media.

TERRITORIAL ISSUES AND HISTORY

We have seen how defining what a Japanese person is might perhaps not be as straightforward as it would first appear. Surely, though, defining the country itself is less problematic? In fact, there are a number of issues even here. In Chapter 1, we already mentioned the issue surrounding discussions of the original islands of Japan. While popularly Japan may be seen in relation to its four main islands, the reality is that it is made up of many hundreds of islands. However, disputes over a number of these point to the problems in defining what the limits of Japan are. But is Japan even where we think it is?

Due to its location, Japan is classified as being in Asia. While this may be accurate in geographic terms, there are problems when associating Japan with Asia in cultural terms. These problems stem from the diversity and size of Asia itself. Whereas we may find commonalities between Japan, South Korea and China, these countries are somewhat different to India, Pakistan or Iraq, for example. To overcome this issue, a more precise description such as 'North East Asia' may be used. While this term helps us to locate Japan within Asia, it is important to keep in mind that Japan is relatively southern in the northern hemisphere when compared to many European nations. That Japan stretches over 3,200km from north to south further complicates matters when trying to place it simply. You may want to have a look at a map of the world and imagine where Japan would be if it were located off the coast of Europe or North America.

In a global context, Japan is often bundled in with the 'East'. But 'East' of where? If the 'North' and 'South' are divided by using the equator, then it is logical to argue that the 'West' and 'East' are divided by using lines of 0° longitude (GMT) and 180° longitude (the International Date Line). However, although this would place Japan in the East, it would also place Germany and much of the rest of Europe in the East. Of course, 'the West' is not about geographical location; it is merely a term of convenience that we all use, but it has no legal basis in itself. It is a term that represents an understanding that the countries within this grouping share certain cultural, political and economic commonalities. However, Japan arguably shares many of these attributes too.

When we consider what and where Japan is, it is important to note that there are a number of territorial disputes that largely relate to unresolved issues dating back to the conclusion of the Second World War. In particular, there are the disputes over the Senkaku Islands, Takeshima Island and four islands (Etorofu, Kunashiri, Shikotan and Habomai) off the coast of Hokkaidō. That I have used the Japanese names for each of these is in itself an issue for some. While an agreed name is desirable, regardless of ownership, the Falkland Islands will always be called Malvinas by Spanish speakers and the English Channel will be called La Manche by the French speakers. So why is South Korea trying to have the Sea of Japan renamed as the East Sea? Why is there a desire to have the internationally recognised name be the one used by a particular country? For the Chinese, the Senkaku Islands are known as Diayou. For the Koreans, Takeshima Island is known as Dokdo, but this island has also been known as Liancourt Rocks in English. The four islands off Hokkaidō are Iturup, Kunashir, Shikotan and Habomai when transcribed from Cyrillic script. Having different names for the same place is clearly confusing, and consistency, at least when speaking a given language, would be preferable. However, the naming issues are, of course, only part of the issue.

Each of these territorial disputes has its own origins and history, which you should familiarise yourself with through additional reading, for example *Peace in Northeast Asia* (Schoenbaum 2008). Here, I would like to emphasise why the issues remain relevant today and why they are seemingly so hard to solve. While many of these islands are themselves very small, ownership of the island also brings with it the 'exclusive economic zone', which extends for 200nm. Not only does this mean extensive fishing grounds, but also, and usually more significantly, it gives access to any natural resources buried below the seabed. So, for example, with Japan having little of its own fossil fuels and China's demand for fossil fuels rising rapidly, the desire to have access to additional resources is great in both countries.

We also cannot overlook the significance of domestic concerns in trying to resolve these disputes. It would be hard for Russia to give up the four disputed islands while it also tries to maintain its influence and control some parts of its own country that have been seeking independence, let alone parts of Ukraine, for example. Due to its lack of natural resources, Japan could offer investment to develop the Siberian oil fields, and these economic demands may help lead to an agreement. In the meantime, no peace treaty has been signed between Japan and Russia to formally end the hostilities of the Second World War. Russia only declared war on Japan, breaking a neutrality agreement, on 8 August 1945, and many of the islands were taken subsequent to Japan's surrender to the Allied Forces. For now, the calls for their return, from right-wing groups in particular, will continue (see Figure 6.2). While right-wing groups make a lot of noise in their vans, few that they pass seem to take interest in their slogans. As we have discussed before, there are times when Japan is far from quiet, but one has to wonder how effective such noisy protests are. Yet while many Japanese will not campaign and protest about some things, as we have seen in Chapter 4, there are clearly exceptions. But perhaps it is not the noisy ones we need to be concerned with. One has to wonder whether the influence reaches politicians and bureaucrats in other more subtle ways. It may be the actions that we cannot see and hear that should be of greater concern.

As well as territorial issues, the legacy of the Second World War can be seen influencing policies and actions in a number of different areas. Perhaps the two that have been the cause for greatest concern – particularly in some of Japan's neighbouring countries that experienced its actions during the war – have been the content of its school history textbooks and the visits to Yasukuni Shrine by leading politicians.

All textbooks have to be authorised by the Ministry of Education, Culture, Sports, Science and Technology (MEXT). Although the system has changed over the years, the principle remains the same. Authors and publishers have to follow certain guidelines and maintain content that fits with the overall national

Figure 6.2 Right-wing protests. To mark the anniversary of the invasion of the Kuril Islands a protest group is allowed to make it way through Kasumigaseki, where many Ministries and the Diet are located. Despite the riot police, the protest is non-violent are relies on shouting statements over loud speakers on the vans.

curriculum, and any book that is intended to be adopted as a textbook has to be screened by a panel of advisors appointed by the Ministry. If a book does not have any required changes made to it, it cannot be expected to be adopted as an official textbook, which is its most likely avenue to be sold successfully. With the Ministry providing textbooks for free to schoolchildren in the compulsory levels of education, it is perhaps not surprising that some say over content is required. However, given the role that education can play in developing ideology, the concern is that the system may become a mechanism to ensure that only content considered desirable by the government will be adopted. While this is unlikely to be an issue in scientific subjects, the handling of aspects of history has the potential to be more problematic. While perhaps not representative of all history textbooks, a number of 'revisionist' books, which attempt to downplay the atrocities committed by Japanese forces, for example, have been approved. However, while it may be disappointing that such books have been successfully approved, one has to wonder how influential they are. While available to be used by boards of education and schools within their jurisdiction, how many use them? If right-wing groups really do have influence 'behind the scenes', why have they not been more successful in pressurising these boards or schools into adopting the revisionist texts?

Another issue where the legacy of the Second World War casts a shadow is in relation to visits to Yasukuni Shrine (see Figure 6.3) by politicians. Yasukuni Shrine itself was initially established to commemorate the victims of the Boshin War (1868–1869), during which supporters of the restoration of the emperor defeated the *shōgun* and his supporters and brought the curtain down on that part of Japan's history. The shrine has gone on to be the place where all those fighting in the name of the emperor have been commemorated. Naturally, this is more controversial for those who were victims of Japanese aggression. This became particularly the case when, in 1978, the shrine included 14 of those executed after they were declared to be war criminals by the International Military Tribunal for the Far East held after the Second World War. Nakasone became the first serving prime minister to visit the shrine when he went on the 40th anniversary of the end of the Second World War. The protests from China and South Korea meant that he did not go again during his tenure, but a number of prime ministers and other politicians have been. But why do they go? Is this a sign of rising nationalism or is it a sign that they want to ensure that the horrors of war are not forgotten and past mistakes are not repeated? Why do the visits usually happen on 15 August, the date of Japan's surrender at the end of the Second World War, rather than on 18 May, the date of the end of the Boshin War? Do the prime ministers have a responsibility to explain, to both Japanese and non-Japanese, the motivations for their visits? Is there a danger that regardless of what they claim to be their motivation, the visit can be interpreted in another way? If the enshrining of the war criminals is problematic, why was this step taken, and can it be undone? Could an alternative memorial that has no potentially religious connections be established? These are just some of the questions that you should be considering as you continue your studies of Japan.

A further area where the legacy of the Second World War and the Constitution, which was established by the Occupation, can be seen relates to defence. According to Article 9 of the Constitution, Japan does not have the right to declare war and that it will not maintain land, sea and air forces. Yet even before the

Figure 6.3 Yasukuni Shrine

Occupation ended, steps were taken to establish a force, called the National Police Reserves. This subsequently evolved into the Self Defence Force (SDF). Although its Japanese name sounds less militaristic than its English equivalent, approximately 1 per cent of the Japanese government's budget is spent on it each year, and so thanks to the development of the economy itself, this means that it has, according to SIPRI (2014), the world's fifth largest budget. Although we need to be careful in making such comparisons, as budgets may not include all the same items in each country and for some countries accurate data may not be provided, the central issue in relation to Japan is how can there be *any* such budget given the wording of the Constitution? Why has the Supreme Court not intervened? Why do more Japanese people not protest about it? However, rather than these questions, the ones that have tended to be the focus of attention for many Japanese have seemingly been questions such as: What are the limits of the SDF? Should the forces be deployed overseas to protect Japanese interests there? Should they be used in UN activities?

Over time, the role of the SDF has evolved and it has even been dispatched overseas. It was the liberation of Kuwait in 1990 and the lack of public acknowledgment that Japan's financial role in funding it rather than providing troops that appeared to create a shift in the position of many politicians. Should Japan continue to expect other countries to put their people's lives on the line when it does not do the same? The Japanese government has seemingly circumnavigated the words of Article 9 through reinterpretation of its essence or through the passing of special provisions. However, some seek reform of the Constitution itself. While opinion polls suggest that many Japanese are in favour of reform of the Constitution in general, there is seemingly greater resistance to changes being made to Article 9 itself. One of the reasons for this would appear to be the legacy of the bombings of Hiroshima and Nagasaki. Although some use these bombings to point to Japan being the victims of the Second World War, the overriding sentiment is that Hiroshima in particular is a symbol of the potential horrors of modern warfare and that this must not be repeated. The 'A-Bomb Dome' (see Figure 6.4), which was a building close to the epicentre of the bomb in Hiroshima, is a visual reminder of the horrors of modern warfare.

Figure 6.4 The A-Bomb Dome. A constant reminder of the horrors of nuclear weapons. Today Hiroshima faces the challenge on ensuring the ruin is preserved and resistant to further erosion or damage from earthquakes without changing its appearance.

Although many Japanese seem resistant to changes being made to Article 9, with some of the proposals made by the Liberal Democratic Party (LDP), we see that rather than abandoning the article, what appears to be sought is a clarification of the limits of the SDF and clarification that Japan would not maintain or use weapons of mass destruction. So why is there still so much resistance to changing Article 9 in particular? Is it that people do not read the proposals? Is it a concern that the government would seek to further reinterpret any new article as the current one has been? Why is it that the focus has been on changing the whole Constitution at once rather than making some amendments to only a handful of articles one by one, starting with some relatively non-controversial ones? In the end, who needs the reform more – Japan or other countries so that they can have greater reassurances about how Japan intends to use its military forces, which seemingly should not even exist?

NATIONALISM IN PRACTICE

While it is perhaps natural to focus upon diplomatic relations, territorial disputes and such like when discussing national and international interests, there are many other ways in which we can see these in action. In Chapter 8, we will be discussing Japan's hosting of large sporting events, such as the Tōkyō 2020 Olympics, as a symbol of Japan's position on the international stage. In this section, let us look at the issue in relation to the production, sale and purchase of certain products.

While it may be Japanese popular culture that has become a central interest for many around the world in the past decade or so, it was arguably Japan's cars and electronics that put Japan firmly on the international stage, boosted its economy and led to a situation where people increasingly saw the need to study Japan and the Japanese language. To help demonstrate this point, please complete Exercise 6.2.

EXERCISE 6.2

Name as many Japanese vehicle manufacturers as you can. Also name as many Japanese electronics companies as you can. Having done this, you may want to try to repeat the exercise for some other countries such as the USA, UK, Germany, France, China and South Korea for comparison.

If we consider car manufacturing, particularly in relation to the discussion in this chapter about nationalism, one question to ask is what do we mean by a Japanese car company or a Japanese car? Is the country of origin of the company most significant? Is the nationality of the CEO significant? Economically, the 'nationality' of a car is determined by where it is manufactured, not the 'nationality' of the company. In other words, a car manufactured by Nissan at its Washington plant in the north-east of England is a British car, and so would be counted as a British export if it were sold to Japan, for example.

The top 10 car manufacturers in the world contain a number of Japanese companies, as you can see in Table 6.1. While we need to be mindful that different companies produce different ranges of cars with different prices to different markets, and the influence exchange rates can have, it appears that the Japanese companies have a lower profit margin than many of their competitors. Seemingly, the motivation for many Japanese companies has been overall sales and market share rather than increased profit and improving efficiency. *Omotenashi*, which was discussed in Chapter 5, is perhaps one part of this. Japanese companies tend to focus on effectiveness rather than efficiency. While in French, for example, these two words are the same (*'efficacité'*), the concepts are quite different. The former stresses the importance of getting the right result, while the latter is about trying to get the result done with the use of as little resources as possible. For a company focused on efficiency, maintaining the same sales but with less staff, for example, would be considered appropriate. This is an approach that seems less pursued by Japanese companies, and the larger they are, the less it seems to be pursued. This helped the development of the 'lifetime employment system' (see Chapter 7).

If we look at your list of Japanese electronics companies from Exercise 6.2, I suspect that there are many household names. However, it is also likely that the list contains many companies that have rebranded or have been forced to make changes in recent years due to the challenges they have been facing from other electronics companies from around the world. However, the nature of both the manufacturing of cars and electronic goods is a complex business, with many components made by smaller, specialist companies. Indeed, I doubt your list of electronics companies included companies such as Toshiba Semi-Conductor and Renesas, which were among the top 10 semi-conductor suppliers in 2013, or Advansat and Tōkyō Electron, which were among the top chip-making equipment suppliers in 2013 (NBR Forum 2014).

While car companies, the electronics industry and Japan's agricultural sector have all benefitted from government support

Table 6.1 The world's top car companies (2013)

Pos	Company	Country	Units produced	Sales ($ billion)	Profit ($ billion)	Profit/ unit ($)
1	Toyota	Japan	10,104,424	224.5	3.4	336
2	General Motors	USA	9,285,425	152.3	6.2	668
3	Volkswagen	Germany	9,254,742	254.0	28.6	3,090
4	Hyundai	South Korea	7,126,413	75.0	7.6	1,066
5	Ford	USA	5,595,483	134.3	5.7	1,019
6	Nissan	Japan	4,889,379	113.7	4.1	839
7	Honda	Japan	4,110,857	96.0	2.6	632
8	Peugeot	France	2,911,764	73.2	−6.7	−2,301
9	Suzuki	Japan	2,893,602	30.4	0.7	242
10	Renault	France	2,676,226	54.5	2.3	859

Source: Table by the author based on information from Yahoo Finance (2013) and Forbes (2014).

in a number of ways over the years (e.g. Okimoto 1989), we cannot overlook the actions of Japanese consumers also. 'Made in Japan' sells well in Japan. Supporting one's own company is natural – although the friends and family discounts offered by some companies should not be ignored also. It would be unimaginable to see a Toyota employee driving a car made by any other manufacturer. The ethos of supporting Japanese interests can perhaps be more extreme than in some other countries. Once I was looking to buy a new camera during a visit to Japan and had narrowed the choice down to two almost identical cameras both made by a Japanese company. I was puzzled, as the lower-spec camera was more expensive than the higher-spec one. When I asked the shop owner why, he pointed out that the lower-spec one was made in Japan rather than in China. When I suggested that the higher price reflected that production costs are higher in Japan, he corrected me to say that in fact virtually all of both cameras were manufactured in China and it was only the final assembly of the higher-spec one that happened in Japan. He said that he charged the higher price for the one made in Japan simply because he knew that many customers would pay extra to have one saying 'Made in Japan' and would prefer this over the features of the camera itself. But as we discussed above, it is not uncommon to overlook the significance of components. I have come across Japanese who will not buy a phone made by Korean company Samsung, but still buy an iPhone, presumably unaware of the parts in it manufactured by Samsung.

These debates again bring us back to the issue as to what defines whether something is 'Chinese', 'South Korean' or 'Japanese'. I have come across some Japanese people who suggest that only Japanese can make top-quality sushi, for example. Why? Can only Italians make pizza and pasta? Why was it that many – most notably non-Japanese who have an interest in Japan from what I experienced – were so concerned about a Chinese woman, Ziyi Zhang, playing the lead role in *Memoirs of a Geisha* (Rob Marshall, 2005), while it has been commonplace for British to play Americans and vice versa in Hollywood movies? It is almost as though some of the strongest Japanese nationalists are non-Japanese who have a love of Japan, and that it is these people who wish Japan to remain unchanged. How would they react if a black athlete were to compete for Japan in a sporting event? Would it be different to how they would react to a black person competing for the UK or USA, for example? Part of the problem in dealing with nationalism and racism in Japan appears to be how non-Japanese also view Japan.

But how long does it take for something to become Japanese? Tempura was developed from a way of cooking introduced into Japan by the Portuguese in the seventeenth century. So it is Portuguese food, or can we say that as the way it has been refined, the ingredients that are now used and the way it is prepared is distinctive enough that it can be considered Japanese? As we discussed in Chapter 5, the service and menu at McDonald's Japan is somewhat different to that found in the UK and USA, so is this a global brand or should we see it as a Japanese company? What about Universal Studios in Ōsaka or Tōkyō Disneyland – are they American or Japanese, or some kind of hybrid?

While the purchase of 'Made in Japan' products may be an easy way to see a form of nationalism or patriotism being practised, sometimes it is not what you can see that is of significance, but what is missing. This is true not just for studying nationalism, but for any aspect of society. Just as we discussed in Chapter 1 the need for you to train your eyes to see the world as a Japanese person may, so you also need to train yourself to look at the whole picture and see what clues there are about the wider context and to look for what is missing. Consider the opening sequence for Universal Pictures films, for example. You can find montages on the Internet (e.g. YouTube 2011a). If you look carefully, you will see that Japan appears to be the only country that tends to get missed. Is this an oversight? Why is it that it has not been included in recent versions despite the company being bought by the Japanese company Panasonic?

Another thing that is seemingly missing in Japan are programmes that make jokes about the imperial family or anything in relation to the bombings of Hiroshima and Nagasaki. The episode of *The Simpsons* that we discussed in Chapter 1 has never been shown in Japan due to, it is suggested, a scene in which Homer Simpson throws the emperor of Japan into a large basket of used *sumō mawashi* belts (Meyer 2007). In 2011, the BBC received an official complaint from the Japanese Embassy in the UK after an episode of the popular comedy quiz programme *QI* used some humour in relation to Tsuomu Yamaguchi who, as the programme questioned, was either one of the luckiest or unluckiest men ever as he was both in Hiroshima for its atomic bombing and in Nagasaki three days later when it was bombed (see YouTube 2011b). That the Japanese government had taken until 2009 to officially recognise Yamaguchi and others as 'double *hibakusha*' (double victims of the atomic bomb) makes it somewhat ironic that official channels should voice any concerns about a sequence that in fact was largely making jokes about the state of British railways and the catering on it (*The Guardian*, 23 January 2011). Perhaps for the embassy, however, it would have been more difficult not to make the complaint than it was to make the complaint. The story was reported in the Japanese media, but they did not explain the contents of the sequence in detail, nor did they explain the context of the programme itself. While the Japanese media did not give the context of this case, in comparison the BBC did its best to give context to an ANA advert that caused some controversy in 2014 (BBC, 22 January 2014), as the report pointed out that the actors who donned a long nose and blond wig to make themselves look more like foreigners were comedians, and that such features are often seen as positive traits in Japan.

In January 2013, the new Boeing 787 Dreamliner suffered a number of problems that led to its grounding globally. ANA was the launch customer for the plane and had 17 planes at the time. In addition, JAL had a further seven planes, meaning that Japanese airlines had nearly half of the 787s being used at the time (BBC, 21 January 2013), so it was unavoidable for the media to link the story with these Japanese airlines. However, while the focus was soon on the batteries as the central problem, the Japanese media appeared to be reluctant to report that these batteries were supplied by a Japanese company. Why would they not report this? Why would they not use their proximity to go and investigate more fully? Were similar forces involved in the way the Japanese media reported the unfolding crisis at the Fukushima Dai-Ichi Nuclear Power Plant in 2011 (see Chapter 8)?

SUMMARY

This chapter has covered a range of complex but important issues. At the heart of the discussions were the need to clarify what we mean by 'the Japanese' and even where and what 'Japan' is. Regardless of how we define nationalism of Japanese, we need to be mindful that an individual's identity is a personal thing, and so regardless of how you or a government may choose to pigeonhole someone, the individual may have a very different view of his or her identity. In this chapter, we have looked at some of the ways in which Japanese 'nationalism' can be seen in action and how this also may have an impact on the way in which Japanese companies, for example, operate.

7

ONE FOR ALL, ALL FOR ONE

Japan is harmonious. One of the most pervasive images of Japanese people is the emphasis on the group ethic. But how accurate is this image? Is it really the case that the individual has no influence? Where, if it exists, does the group orientation get developed? If the Japanese are so harmonious and cooperative, how could there be any crime in Japan? What role do the police have and how do we explain the existence of the *Yakuza*, Japan's notorious crime syndicates? These are just some of the questions and issues that we will be addressing in this chapter. In doing this, we will be looking at a range of aspects of Japanese society and popular culture, and how they either confirm or undermine some of the stereotypes about the role and workings of the individuals and groups in Japan.

DEVELOPING GROUPS

In Chapter 6, we discussed how schools are seen as a critical in developing many aspects of an individual's ideologies in relation to nationalism. However, they are also central in development of behaviour. With children often spending much of the day at school, and then possibly going on to *juku* ('cram schools'), let alone additional time spent at schools during weekends and holidays for club activities, there is ample opportunity for the school to develop behaviour. The lack of time at home also reduces some of the opportunities for parents to influence their children.

Group activities are commonplace in schools. With class sizes in many schools being around 36 children, it becomes difficult for teachers to give attention to individual children, and so it is not uncommon for exercises to require groups of six children to work together. However, teachers may try to develop groups and subgroups that are made up of children with varying abilities so that they experience things that help them develop skills in cooperation (see Cave 2007). It is not only during the classes that the groups can be seen in action. At lunchtime, children will eat in their classroom. One group of the class will be responsible for going to collect the food, which is often cooked off site and brought to the school where it will be kept warm by the kitchen staff. Once back at the classroom, the group will then be responsible for serving up the food and distributing the trays. As the main food will often consist of rice and some other hot food in separate containers, the children will need to judge that they are giving out an amount that is both sufficient but also ensures that there is enough for the whole class. After lunch, the classroom and school will be cleaned by the children, with each group having its own designated area to keep clean. The leader of the group will be varied over time. Rather than ordering the other children in the group what to do, their role often focuses on reminding the others on what needs to be done and trying to motivate them to do it well. However, I have also seen some more bossy styles.

Club activities form an important part of school life. Children will only be a member of one club, and the choice of clubs can vary from school to school. As the clubs will have at least one teacher that helps oversee the activities, although the teacher may not always be present and he or she may leave it to the children to organise some of the sessions, clubs at some schools will reflect the interests and skills of individual teachers. While this means that each school in a city may have a somewhat different profile, choice of school is primarily decided on the basis of which school is closest to the child's home, and so there are no guarantees that the school a child goes to will have the activity that he or she would be most interested in. Although public schools are co-educational, the sports clubs are segregated by gender and each sport is usually only available for either boys or girls. The sports clubs, in particular, will sometimes meet in the morning before classes for a practice session. Schools will generally not have changing rooms or showers, so children will get changed in front of the rest of the class in their classroom. After classes, clubs will meet on most days. Again, the sports clubs will often be practice sessions focused on developing certain skills. Match play is rare, and matches against clubs from other schools, at least at elementary and lower secondary schools, are unusual too. Although public schools no longer have classes on Saturdays, it is common for many clubs to meet on a Saturday at the school. Similarly, during the holidays, the school remains open and there will be club activities. Teachers will also be on site, both to help at their clubs but also for meetings or to do other work.

In all clubs, there is a strong emphasis on all members working together and each individual trying his or her best. While in sports it may be easy to imagine how this operates, in other clubs, such as the English-speaking society, the initial cooperative element may be in deciding upon a theme for the club to concentrate on for a term before each individual, usually with at least one other child, then works on particular things. The clubs cut across years, so it is natural that there is a mixture of abilities. Although the emphasis largely appears to be on raising everyone's ability through hard work, the nature of how this is achieved can vary greatly from club to club. The baseball club, the members of which are usually distinguishable by their crew-cut haircuts, has traditionally been the one where the work ethic has been most severe, and so bullying has been seen as a problem.

Bullying has been seen as a particular problem in Japan, and, as in most countries, can take a variety of forms, and the nature that an individual may experience could include any number of them, whether it be name calling, extortion or more physical forms. What may be different is that teachers may not always actively try to stop the bullying. Is this part of the training that the group comes first and individuals come second? It is often the weaker, quieter children that will become the focus for the bullies. Stronger, more vocal and sometimes more disruptive students are rarely the attention for bullying by the group. In this respect, the much-cited Japanese concept that 'the nail that sticks out gets hammered down' is not accurate. Bullying was thought to have become such a problem in the 1980s following some incidents of children being driven to suicide that the Ministry of Education began recording the number of incidents of bullying and trying to develop policies to deal with it. The number of cases has seen fluctuations over the years, but whatever the recorded level, it is unlikely that they reflect the true number of cases and many more go unreported. Changes in the reported level are likely to reflect the fact that certain cases may be reported in the media and focus national attention on the problem, and this may encourage both further reporting of cases, as well as lead, at least briefly, to renewed attempts to deal with it.

HARMONY AND UNIFORMITY

It is not only bullying where there may be statistical problems. Crime rates may also suffer from a similar problem of under-reporting. When compared to many other industrialised countries, the rates of most crimes are noticeably low. It is tempting to look for aspects of Japanese culture that explain this. Could it be due to the group orientation and cooperation that develops at the school level, so that the individual does not seek personal gain at the expense of others? Could it be due to the close-knit nature of Japanese neighbourhoods, so that it is hard for someone to come into an area and not be noticed? Is it due to the placing of staffed police boxes throughout towns and cities, so that there is a constant visual reminder that there are police nearby? Each of these may help. But what if the Japanese are not reporting the crimes in the first place? What if the feeling of guilt or shame that such a thing had happened to them or concerns about the impact of reporting it are so great that the police do not even come to know of the crime being committed? I have even come across a Japanese person not reporting a crime as they did not want the perpetrator to get into trouble, instead seeking justice through a compensation payment. What if the police do not act upon incidents and record them unless they are confident that the perpetrator will be found? What if society and politicians do not send out a message that certain activities are heinous crimes? What does a politician, such as Seiichi Ōta in 2003 describing gang rapists as 'vigorous' and 'close to normal' (BBC, 27 June 2003), tell us about Japan and the state of its apparent safe, harmonious society?

Although official statistics may not reflect the true level of crimes in Japan, there is no doubt that on the whole, Japan is a safe country. If you were to drop a wallet, it is likely that it would be handed into a police box or left for you to collect. Similarly, items left on a train are likely to be left alone and be collected by cleaners or by train staff and taken to a lost property office. Japanese cities do not generally suffer from having areas where crime is so rife that one cannot feel safe walking alone through it. As you continue your studies of Japan, you should explore what may have led to this situation. But you should also be mindful to look out for whether things are changing, and if so, what may be causing these changes.

When it comes to discussing crime in Japan, however, there is one area that garners particular interest internationally, and that is the *Yakuza*, which is formally referred to as *bōryokudan* ('gangster organisation'). While they may be referred to as the Japanese mafia, the way in which they are allowed to exist and operate would suggest that this analogy is not very helpful. However, I do not propose to discuss the activities of the *Yakuza* here, but rather to focus on the different image that appears to exist of them outside of Japan compared to within Japan. To do this, please complete Exercise 7.1 (overleaf) first.

The most pervasive image of the *Yakuza* in English-speaking countries is of tattooed men, many of whom may be missing a finger, which has been cut off by the individual himself to atone for some wrongdoing (*yubitsume*). This is the image that has been enforced through Hollywood films such as *The Yakuza* (Sydney Pollack, 1974) and *Black Rain* (Ridley Scott, 1989). But for most Japanese, the *Yakuza* are violent thugs involved in extortion, drug trafficking and prostitution. Although the *Yakuza* may portray themselves as Japan's modern-day Robin Hoods, and there are some who romanticise their image, for most Japanese their image is probably less glamorous or intriguing than the one

---

EXERCISE 7.1

Go to an Internet search engine and type in the word *Yakuza*. Once the results come up, select the option to show only images. Scan through the images and make a note of what some of the key features are. Keep in mind also the discussion in Chapter 6 about what may be missing from the images. Having looked through a good number of images, then go to http://en.wikipedia.org/wiki/Yakuza and copy the Japanese script for *Yakuza* (ヤクザ). Paste this text into the search box for the Japanese version of the search engine and again select the images tab. As before, scan through the images and make a note of some of the key features of them and also what is missing.

---

in English-speaking countries. While it is certainly the case that the *Yakuza* can be instrumental in ensuring that *matsuri* (local festivals often linked to Shintō shrines) are successfully run and have been quick to provide logistical and other aid after major earthquakes, this does not detract from the fact that they are, ultimately, criminals who strike fear into most Japanese.

In looking through the images of the *Yakuza*, one thing that you may have noticed was the apparent uniformity of how they look: the tattoos, the hairstyles and the clothing. Uniformity of appearance is a key part of the group mechanism in Japan. Buruma points out that:

> the Japanese, on a whole, like to be identified and categorised according to their group or occupation, rather simply as individuals. No Japanese cook worth his salt would want be seen without his tall white hat; 'interis' (intellectuals) sport berets and sunglasses, like 1920s exiles on the Left Bank of Paris.
>
> (Buruma 2001: 70)

However, the uniformity of uniforms is not always a matter of volition. If it were, why are so many posters and signs needed in company buildings reminding employees of the appropriate dress? While the levels of detail for length of skirt, style of hair and such like that are found at Japanese schools may not be uncommon to schools around the world, the requisites relating to hair and jewellery that I have seen in some of the railway companies, for example, would be, at best, unpopular in many European countries, and perhaps even illegal in some cases. For many *Yakuza*, having tattoos can be problematic, as many *onsen* resorts will not permit those with tattoos to enter. But this pigeonholing points to a fundamental problem with taking uniformity to its logical conclusion: not all people who have tattoos are *Yakuza*. There are many non-Japanese who have tattoos and who may not be allowed to enter a hot spring because of this, despite not seemingly being *Yakuza*. And how are former *Yakuza* meant to live a normal life and go to places such as hot springs if they are being judged on their appearance?

Uniformity is not restricted to how people dress. The academic year starts at the same time for all across the country in April. But this start date has implications due its lack of uniformity with many other countries, as it makes it harder to arrange periods of international exchange at universities, for example. Although there has been discussion about changes being made, at least at the university level, progress is difficult. There are practical reasons for this – what would students do for the six months between leaving upper secondary school and starting university? With many Japanese companies, particularly the large ones, only recruiting en masse in April, there would be a need to address the potential need for two recruitment periods depending on whether people were entering from university or from upper secondary school. But there may also be symbolic reasons. Pictures of new students, whether it be at school or university, entering the grounds for the first time past the main gate surrounded by cherry blossom is a pervasive one. Yet such an image is not a sign of the uniformity of Japan, but rather the dominance of Tōkyō in particular. The cherry blossom comes out much earlier in the year in Okinawa and not until May in Hokkaidō. The idea that the start of the school year coincides with the start of spring, which is seen as when new life starts, is overly simplistic – after all, the flowers of the *Camellia Japonica* (*tsubaki*) come out in winter, for example.

The apparent uniformity within companies, as well as the mass recruitment of new employees in April, means that Japan does not have a labour market as it would be understood in many other countries. The lifetime employment system is a well-known aspect of Japanese companies. However, its significance may be somewhat overstated. This system has only ever applied to *some* of those working in larger companies. Furthermore, if you go to work for a company in the UK or USA, for example, unless on a fixed-term contract, is not the assumption that you could stay there for life if you so choose? The difference with Japan, however, has seemingly been the reluctance to restructure and fire people. Poor workers may be retained and kept as *madogiwazoku* (people by the window), doing menial tasks with no prospect of promotion. This system may lead people to be risk averse. To try something different and then fail is likely to have implications, while success is not necessarily rewarded since, particularly historically, Japanese companies have not had performance-related pay, bonuses have not been linked to an individual's performance and promotions may have owed more to age than job performance. Better to keep your head down and get on with the job than risk drawing attention to yourself seems to have been an attitude adopted by many. Employees also seemingly do not look to leave the company and seek better pay and opportunities elsewhere. The chances to do so are also thought to be limited as the cultures of companies are thought to be so different that fitting into a new company in a similar sector, despite the skills, knowledge and experience they may have, is not possible. The two-way 'loyalty' between these large companies and some of their employees is reinforced through subsidised housing and other benefits. However, with Japanese companies having to respond to more and more global economic challenges, things may be changing, and it is important for you to keep an eye on these trends and not rely on the simplified stereotypical view of how businesses operate.

The loyalty between organisations and employees can also be seen when something goes wrong. During the decision-making process, everyone will have an opportunity to express his or her view. This may lead to situations where there is a discussion and, where necessary, a compromise and agreed position can be reached. However, perhaps more frequently, the discussion is merely an airing of views. There may be limited discussion and little attempt to change individuals' views. Changing of views is seemingly achieved through a process of self-reflection upon hearing the opinions of others. Self-reflection can be a time-consuming process and so decision-making processes can also take some time in Japan. The result of the discussions, however, will be one that all parties can be claimed to have had the opportunity to be a part of, and so all are expected to unite behind it. Consequently, should something go wrong, it is rarely the responsibility of the individual, but the group and organisation as a whole. It may be that a public apology will be needed, and in such cases this will be done by an individual on behalf of all. The apology, the bow and possibly even a resignation are seen as a symbolic gesture of the actions of the whole, and not a sign that he or she was personally to blame. He or she is unlikely to face any recriminations him or herself. It will be the company or organisation that will be investigated, if the case is that severe. Compare this to societies where individuals may see a company at fault and try to take action against a company as a whole, but it is not uncommon for an individual to be found responsible and to be fired or otherwise sanctioned.

HIERARCHY

Given the discussions in the previous section about uniformity and individuals working together within a group, it may surprise you to then have a section entitled 'Hierarchy'. However, there is a structure to Japanese society. Uniformity and the spirit of togetherness that is perhaps seen as a result of group dynamics is found within parts of the structure rather than across all of society. There can be conflict. But there are many times when conflict is avoided not due to positive actions, but seemingly rather due to different parts of society and the structure either avoiding any interaction at all or by playing what at times can seem quite an elaborate game of social interaction.

In relation to how these interactions work, the concept that has been regarded as particularly helpful is that of the distinction between *uchi* and *soto* (Hendry 2012: 42–4). *Uchi* is literally the inside, while *soto* is the outside. Whether one is interacting with another person from part of the *uchi* – this could be another from your group in the company, someone else from within the company, a friend or a member of the family – will depend on the context and situation. Indeed, the same person could be part of the *soto* in a different situation. At the heart of the *uchi/soto* dichotomy is trust. Trust is gained, but being introduced by a person who is already part of the *uchi* effectively provides a shortcut to becoming part of the *uchi*. It is for this reason that the choice of university and clubs there can be important, as the networks developed within can be beneficial when it comes to finding employment, for example. The way in which people will talk to one another and any others present will depend on the *uchi/soto* relationship. The Japanese language itself changes, with honorific, polite, plain and humble forms to help with ensuring there is no mistaking how individuals view the relationships between each other. It is not only the language that will reflect the nature of the relationship, as the degree to which one bows will also be a sign of this. Of course, in an international environment, there are times when those who typically use other forms of greetings will be interacting with the Japanese. Should you shake hands and bow, or just do one or the other, depending perhaps on where you are? In a visit to the Imperial Palace in 2009, President Obama both shook hands and bowed. While viewed as perfect diplomacy by some, there were also others, particularly back in the USA, who saw the bow as a sign of him kowtowing to the emperor (BBC, 10 February 2010). Given how most Japanese tend, traditionally at least, not to be tactile in public, one wonders what the reaction would be of a Japanese prime minister greeting a leading politician with kisses on both cheeks, as is customary in some countries.

The gauging of distance between people leads to what Hendry (1995) refers to as 'wrapping'. In some cases, this wrapping is very literal. The wrapping of a gift can be as significant as the contents itself, and its unwrapping will rarely be done in public so as to avoid any potential problems if the receiver shows disappointment, or, when gifts are exchanged, there is a clear and inappropriate difference in the beauty or cost of the gifts. However, the wrapping can also be metaphorical. The way in which the language is used to wrap the actual contents of the exchange is just one example of this. The situation itself can also be wrapped. For example, there are likely to be spaces where visitors (*soto*) to a company can be hosted rather than the meeting being held where the person usually works (*uchi*). The meeting room itself is likely to follow a prescribed design that helps provide a common understanding of where people should sit. Such wrapping avoids any potential unease or conflict.

But there are other things that may also aid individuals in understanding their relative positions. As status has traditionally been gained through seniority rather than past performance, there is a prevalence in Japan to ask people's age and, for example in the media, for the age to routinely be given in brackets after an individual's name. The exchange of business cards (*meishi*) is another factor in aiding the interaction. While the person's age is unlikely to be displayed, their role within a company or organisation will be. Knowing whether the person is a section chief or a manager will quickly enable the receiver of the card to understand that person's relative position in the hierarchy within the company.

If you are involved in discussions with a Japanese person, consequently, you need to be aware that even if the conversation is happening in English, your counterpart may well still be interacting according to the social intercourse with which they are accustomed. While it can be relatively simple to adjust to the 'wrapping', how the distinctions of *soto* and *uchi* work, and hierarchical structures, there is a further connected issue that can be more problematic. In order to maintain good relations, or at least maintain a situation where a relationship can continue, most Japanese are apt to say things that, in essence, they believe the other person would like to hear. However, such words may not actually be an expression of what they actually think or believe. Those who start studying and using Japanese are often praised on how good their Japanese is. In reality, while there may be an admiration in the person trying to learn and use what even many Japanese people themselves believe to be a difficult language, they may not be thinking the person's Japanese is good at all. However, expressing the compliment not only encourages the person to keep trying, a concept that many Japanese value, but makes it easier to maintain good relations with the other person. This difference between what is expressed (*tatemae*) and what the person actually believes (*honne*) can be seen as deceitful, but equally its use to help maintain even fragile relationships can often be commendable when the alternatives are considered.

So given the existence of *tatemae*, one has to be careful when concluding a Japanese person is kind. Kindness and politeness are not the same. Even politeness has cultural-specific elements to it. If you were to trip in the street in Japan, you may not find that anybody comes to your aid. To do so would be to admit that they saw you trip, or at least the consequences of the trip, and that in itself may be a cause of greater embarrassment than if you thought that nobody had seen the incident. That they have intervened with a stranger would also cause issues in terms of trying to place the relationship in terms of *uchi/soto* and social (by which we often mean age in relation to Japan) hierarchy. While giving up a seat for an elderly passenger, someone with a disability, a pregnant woman or someone carrying a child may be referred to as being 'polite', in Japan it may be seen as an act of kindness. An act of kindness usually carries with it the idea that the receiver is then obligated to repay the kindness. Between friends or in work situations, there are many opportunities to do this, but with a stranger on a train this could be more problematic. It is not unusual for such an act of kindness to be refused or to be met with a seemingly overly long conversation in which thanks are expressed. I have even been given a gift in such a situation. So returning to *omotenashi*, which we discussed in Chapter 5, is this an act of kindness that the company, for example, expects to be repaid through repeat business? A restaurant providing a space where a large bottle of *sake*, *shōchū* (a Japanese liquor) or whisky can be kept could be seen as a form of *omotenashi* and kindness, in that the customer has not felt obligated to finish it at one visit. However, by keeping the bottle on display with the person's name clearly on display may also develop a feeling of obligation, or enforced loyalty, upon the person to return at a later date.

Loyalty and trust are concepts that we have touched upon throughout this chapter. Indeed, although perhaps not explicitly, they are concepts that have been in the background throughout much of the book. Is Japan really so unusual in seeing these as positive attributes? Probably not. But what may be at times different in Japan are the degrees to which it shapes the workings of society, the way in which it is rewarded, the extremes that some may go to in the name of loyalty and the greater potential impact that it may have on both individuals and society. Given our discussions of symbolism in the book, it is only appropriate to give mention here to perhaps Japan's most well-known symbol of loyalty: Hachikō. Hachikō was a dog that, after his owner died at work, continued to go to the station every day to wait for his owner as he had done previously. After the dog eventually died, he was immortalised with a statue outside the station, Shibuya, and today it is probably Japan's most famous meeting point (see Figure 7.1). Indeed, it is so popular and busy at times that it can be hard to see the statue itself. The story of Hachikō, or Chūken Hachikō ('faithful dog Hachikō'), as he is often referred, was turned into a film in 1987 in Japan, *Hachikō Monogatari* (Seijirō Kōyama). An American remake was subsequently made with a US-based version of the story still using an Akita dog and a variant of the original's name, *Hachi: A Dog's Tale* (Lasse Hallström, 2009).

If we focus upon loyalty among humans, an example of extreme version is perhaps the story of Hirō Onoda who continued to hide in the jungle of the Philippines and 'fight' the war, refusing to believe that Japan had surrendered some 30 years earlier until he received a personal communication to lay down his arms from the emperor (Onoda 2013). While even Onoda reflected that he had been a fool (*The Independent*, 17 January 2014), the loyalty shown by both soldiers and samurai before them is a trait that many Japanese aspire towards. Indeed, the thought that this quality is missing in the younger generation, as demonstrated by their more selfish behaviour (see below), is suggested as one of the reasons why some war films and TV dramas have been particularly popular. However, as Kirsch (2014) points out, the theme of some of these – through the use of time travel or the swapping of characters – is to point out that the values exist today too, albeit sometimes hidden beneath the surface.

While there may be cases where Japan appears to reward loyalty more than some other societies, perhaps what is of greater significance has been the punishing of lack of loyalty. Let us consider here the implications for family life. With the additional pressure that there are certain expectations that are to be met, marriage, for example, can be the result of obligations for a man

Figure 7.1 Hachikō

and woman to be together and to procreate to continue to the family line. Concepts of love and happiness seem to play a smaller role, at least historically. While divorce rates have risen, and are perhaps higher than many Japanese believe them to be, there would appear to be some remaining stigma associated with divorce. That some choose to get a *shigo rikon* ('post-death divorce'), whereby they refuse to be buried or memorialised with their former partner, is perhaps an indication of just the tip of the iceberg of those who remain in a marriage that they wish they were not part of. The expectation to marry and procreate has been a particular issue for Japan's homosexuals, many of whom choose to hide their true feelings in order to maintain the loyalty to their family, although they may continue homosexual practices in secret.

So far, this chapter has stressed the significance of the group in Japan and some of the sacrifices an individual may make in order to maintain loyalty, trust and harmony. However, as already pointed out, the system does not totally ignore the individual. Despite this, there are suggestions (e.g. Woronoff 1980: 36; Duke 1986: 27) that existence outside of the group is difficult and could risk 'severe psychological problems' (Buruma 2001: 100). Yet the ability to 'sway with the breeze' is something that most Japanese learn to do as the improvement of the group in turn improves the individual (Duke 1986: 33, 193–4). But on top of this, Reischauer and Jansen (1995: 159) point out that the individual in Japan 'retains a very strong self-identity' and they are 'not a nation of lemmings' (Duke 1986: 193).

While we have already noted how the individual's views will generally be respected in meetings, the individual's power can be seen in more concrete ways elsewhere. Many visitors to Japan still arrive at Narita International Airport. One of the more puzzling sights to greet arriving planes are the houses that taxiways navigate around in the middle of the airport complex. The location of the second runway is even out of alignment with the rest of the airport due to the refusal of one farmer to sell his land. The houses and farms are there because the individual refused to give up his or her land. There is nothing that can be done about it. I have seen many other examples of construction work that has only been part completed due to such protests. While eventually the person may be persuaded to move, the fact remains that there are cases where the individual has power.

So far, this chapter has emphasised the way in which groups of individuals may operate together while acknowledging that the individual can have power of his or her own at times. The concept of *uchi/soto* has provided a mechanism to explain why some individuals will cooperate with each other, while members of that group will have a different dynamic when dealing with another group. But what happens when individuals who do not know each other, but who may share a common interest, meet? Introductions tend to be done through a mutual acquaintance, but what if no such person is available? Will the two people interact and potentially collaborate, or not? I hope by this stage you realise that there is not going to be a single response to this question, as not all Japanese people behave in exactly the same way all of the time. While we may be able to make some generalisations, we need to acknowledge that there are going to be exceptions to these. If I had set up the situation above as being a situation where it is people who can clearly be seen to have a common interest in photography are meeting, would the answer to the question be any different? Does the fact that they are photographers, identifiable from the equipment they are carrying, mean that there is some form of common *uchi*? Does the apparent collaborative nature of Japanese people mean that they would work together? Or do the problems of how to interact with strangers still have precedence? Again, I would suggest we cannot give an answer that covers *all* Japanese. In my time of going to photograph *shinkansen*, for example, I have found that there is very little interaction between others who take such pictures. Pointing out a good photo spot is not appreciated. At stations, where there may be limited space, this does not mean that there will be any collaboration. There appears to be a focus on achieving their goal of getting the perfect shot by themselves, regardless of others. For some examples of this, see RocketNews24 (4 January 2014). Of course, not all train photographers are like this, but the nature of many such photographers contrasts with many of those who take pictures of planes, where I have found that there is much greater interaction between apparent strangers, although there are exceptions here too. So be careful of making any generalisations about how 'the Japanese' behave.

POPULAR CULTURE

Having discussed the relative significance of the group and individual in Japan generally, let us turn now to look at popular culture in Japan to test how the group/individual dynamic plays out. In doing so, we will also discuss the wider significance of

Japanese popular culture in terms of developing Japan's national and international image, one of the themes that is central to this book.

If we consider trends in popular culture, looking at what people wear, where they visit or what they purchase may provide insights into what group(s) people belong to or how they behave more individualistically. What you can see in action are the concepts of *soto* and *uchi*. However, it may not be possible to fully appreciate the distinctions until a group is in a situation where it is interacting with another group, for example. But we also need to be careful not to oversimplify. A group of football supporters may all be wearing a replica of the club shirt, but on careful examination you may find that individuals are wearing strips from different seasons. There is conformity to a degree, but there are also differences, however subtle they may be.

Where should we draw the line between the group and the individual with some activities? Returning to Shibuya again, there are many places for people to go for *karaoke*. These are typically frequented by a group that will go to a room to sing along to the backing music of their favourite tracks. While the act of going together is very much a group activity, for the most part it will be an individual or duo that will sing. During this time, he or she will be allowed to perform his or her choice of song. While in some cases there may be a degree of commonality of choice of songs due to the interests of the group, it need not be this way. It would be unusual for the group to join in with the singing, as I have often observed in countries such as the UK. The group will offer support through clapping and cheering at appropriate moments, but the individual is allowed his or her moment to perform. So is this a group activity or an individual activity done in the company of others?

You can see similar issues in many Japanese sports. Consider, for example, *sumō*, which appears to be an individual sport, as at any one time there are only two people (*rikishi*) fighting against each other. However, each *rikishi* is organised into *heya* (a stable), which is overseen by an *oyakata*. The structure is perhaps reminiscent of what is seen in the hierarchical structure of the *Yakuza*. The *heya* provides the location for training, and until the *rikishi* reaches the professional level, which many do not reach, it is also where they will live and eat too. The fellow *rikishi* are the support mechanism by which individuals improve, and without a strong *heya* even the most talented and hard-working *rikishi* are likely to struggle. The group element is far from insignificant.

But returning to an issue we have previously touched upon, what do we mean by Japanese? Is even *sumō* Japanese? Has the increase in the numbers of non-Japanese impacted the popularity of the sport, and if so, why? Can foreign *rikishi* take part in all of the elements of *sumō* and perform all elements of the rituals in the way that a Japanese person would? Are the actions of a non-Japanese scrutinised and commented on more than if a Japanese *rikishi* acted in the same way? Would a *rikishi* with tattoos be acceptable? Would someone with blonde hair be expected to dye it black? Without doubt, there has been a rise in the significance of non-Japanese *rikishi* over the past two decades, and many tournaments are won by non-Japanese. But perhaps this is not a bad thing. For years, some Japanese referred to the 'Wimbledon-isation' of British industry, drawing a parallel with the lack of success by British people at the Wimbledon tennis tournament. Instead, Britain was the location where other nationalities were able to perform well (with the establishment of Japanese factories being a reason for Japanese interest in this respect). However, with victories at the Olympics in 2012 and the men's singles championship in 2013, Wimbledon is once again a place where British players have succeeded. Perhaps *sumō* is going through its own period of 'Wimbledon-isation', before a new wave of Japanese *rikishi* come to the fore again.

While there is a group element to even seemingly individual sports, the reading of *manga* and watching of *anime* is a much more individual pursuit. However, as we saw in Figure 3.2, there are examples where *manga* or *anime* are part of a much larger marketing operation that can include TV programmes, non-*anime* films, electronic games and such like. With the film industry looking for new, original storylines (Rikei Kubo, interview, August 2010), popular *manga* and *anime* are an obvious source. The development of the games industry, whether it be electronic or some other form, has helped bring a group element to the consumption of popular *manga* and *anime* as individuals come to play with other individuals and groups of fans of particular *manga* and *anime* so that they can find additional ways to interact with each other beyond discussing the storylines, for example. But with the development and usage of the Marvel Comics brand, for example, is Japan really so different?

Looking at many aspects of Japanese popular culture, one of the key elements appears to be the importance of cute (*kawaii*) things. In many respects, perhaps the market leader and greatest symbol of this are Sanrio and their character Hello Kitty (see Figure 7.2). Although Sanrio has many other principal characters, it is Hello Kitty that has not only been its most successful in Japan, but also globally. Due to its backstory, which I will let you check for yourself, and lack of obviously Japanese features, it is questionable to what degree some are aware that the Hello Kitty brand originated in Japan. But for our study of Japan, what is key is how Hello Kitty can be seen both as an example of the power of cute, but also just how far Japan is prepared to develop and use a particular character. Hello Kitty seemingly can appear anywhere and on anything. She has even been used as a tourism ambassador (*Anime* News Network 2008), along with other characters such as Doraemon (*The Japan Times*, 20 April 2013) and robots (*The Japan Times*, 20 March 2014a).

With sales in excess of ¥100 billion per year, Hello Kitty has helped to promote Sanrio as being one of Japan's most successful companies. A visit to Sanrio Puroland, a relatively small indoor theme park, can help in revealing the popularity of Hello Kitty and the other characters, the types of people who like these characters, the different ways in which companies will seek to get revenue and such like. However, watching the shows also reveals something of the ethos of Sanrio, which itself appears to reflect core values in Japanese society. In one show, a character has to work with another to ensure that a star is returned to space, and the storyline deals with issues of selfishness, the need to avoid arguments and the importance of telling the truth. In another show, it is Hello Kitty who teaches a king the importance of spending more time with the queen, who has been left behind as he goes on a golf trip. There are probably a number of viewing parents with whom this storyline will strike a chord.

Figure 7.2 Hello Kitty. A mother and children interacting with a Hello Kitty model in a Japanese tea ceremony mock-up at Sanrio Puroland.

It is important to be aware that 'cute' is not something only for female consumers. Even Sanrio has launched ranges, such as its *shinkansen* range, which was both cute and primarily aimed at boys. On top of this, there is no shortage of '*tarento*' (celebrities), actresses and singers who are promoted due to their ability to appeal to those boys and men who like 'cute'. At an extreme, this has also been linked with a Lolita complex, which appears to be relatively widespread in Japan, particularly if the popularity of certain *manga* and *anime* reflect the tastes of their readers (Kinsella 2000). This is not to say that beauty is any less a marketing tool in the media than in many other countries around the world. Is this why Japanese female singers tend to have such a short career? Is this why multi-member female pop group AKB48 has been so successful – as it had so many people that there was somebody to seemingly suit almost all, and it developed a system that would allow the group to continuously reincarnate itself? To learn more about these subjects, read *Idols and Celebrity in Japanese Media Culture* (Galbraith and Karlin 2012). Of course, the success of pop acts should not merely be about looks, as the quality of the music is also significant, as are the female fans. But in studying Japan, we need to try to find out what is happening behind the scenes and understand what marketing mechanisms are being used, and why, in trying to get consumers to part with their money.

So let us return to the issues pertinent to this chapter. Is popular culture a group activity or an individual activity? There is probably no single answer to this. Even individuals who seem to live almost only for their hobby, now known around the world by the Japanese word *otaku*, may still interact with other *otaku*. Japan expects interaction of individuals. Those that do not and who shut themselves off from society, *hikikomori*, are seen as abnormal. Would it be any different in any other country?

SUMMARY

In this chapter, we have covered a range of issues in relation to the group and the individual in Japan. We have looked at how the group ethos is developed from a young age and that the education system is particularly important. However, this chapter has also emphasised that the Japanese individual is perhaps not only more powerful than many outside Japan realise, but that he or she may at times be even more powerful than his or her 'Western' counterparts, for example. As Reischauer and Jansen (1995: 128–9) point out, the reality is that Japan and the West 'are much less different than the American Lone Ranger myth, for example, or the traditional Japanese ideal of selfless merging with the group would lead one to believe'. The chapter concluded by giving you just a few insights into how you can see elements of Japanese individual and group behaviour by looking at aspects of Japanese popular culture. I hope that this will encourage you to further explore this in relation to any aspects of Japanese pop culture that particularly interest you.

8

(RE)BUILDING JAPAN

Japan is discordant. While we have discussed in the previous chapter about the drive to harmony among the people who live in the country, the land on which they live provides a number of challenges. We have already mentioned some of the seasonal issues that impact Japan and that these can lead to considerable damage and loss of life. However, as single events, it is earthquakes that provide the greatest challenge. This chapter will look at how Japan responds to these challenges and potential disasters. These discussions will tie together many of the points raised throughout the book in relation to the way in which people and organisations in Japan behave. This chapter will further look at the media reporting and consider the problems of understanding events in Japan through the use of both Japanese and foreign media. The chapter will show how the responses to disasters and how they are portrayed in the media is about building and rebuilding Japan, both in the literal sense when reconstruction, for example, is needed, but also in terms of building an image of Japan. To further demonstrate this argument, the chapter will conclude by looking at Japan's desire to host major international events as a means to help construct an image of Japan on the global stage, and how this even got linked to the rebuilding after the Great East Japan Earthquake of 2011.

WHAT IS A DISASTER?

11 March 2011 is a day that has gone down in infamy, or at least world history, as the original version of Roosevelt's famous speech was written. For a day, the world turned its attention to events as they were beamed live to screens. Social media went into overdrive as all seemed to have something to say about what they were seeing. The conclusion of many, including the news networks, which themselves seemed to be sucked to new low levels of reporting quality, was that it was like a scene out of a Hollywood movie. This, of course, totally missed the point. What we were watching was reality. It is the Hollywood movies that have over time managed to find a means to reproduce the true horror of these devastating events. As one event, the earthquake, was over, so others, tsunami, came. When that seemed to be over, so the problems shifted to events at the Fukushima Dai-Ichi Nuclear Power Plant. Seemingly never before had a tragedy had so many different elements. Never before had it been so well filmed. But did all understand what they were seeing? Did the state and people respond appropriately?

First, to understand how Japan responds to earthquakes, we need to ensure that we comprehend what is involved. There are three factors in an earthquake: intrinsic (magnitude, type, location), geologic (type of soil, distance from the event) and societal (conditions of construction and preparation). Furthermore, there are direct effects (the fault itself, which may produce little damage to buildings) and secondary effects (the seismic waves, which cause most of the damage). The primary wave associated with the earthquake itself travels quickly and can be detected, giving time for some systems to send out warnings so preparations can be made before the more destructive secondary waves hit some seconds later. Indeed, in Japan, a network of sensors are in place so that warning can be sent out to the public and also so that the *shinkansen* can be slowing down or stop before the more damaging secondary wave strikes. The only time a *shinkansen* has ever derailed due to an earthquake was when it was passing so close to the epicentre of the earthquake itself that there was too little time to slow it down. However, even then there were no significant injuries (Hood 2006a: 169). The concern about the potential impact on the Tōkaidō Shinkansen has also been one of the motivating factors for JR Tōkai to build the linear *shinkansen* between Tōkyō and Ōsaka. Although the initial section will be between Tōkyō and Nagoya, this route, with trains operating up to 500km/h, will provide a safer option, due to its location and construction, in terms of earthquake resistance, as well as an alternative, should the Tōkaidō Shinkansen ever be unusable.

While it is common to speak of the Richter scale in relation to earthquakes, the differences due to the intrinsic, geologic and societal nature of earthquakes means that the system does not explain why some earthquakes become a disaster. An earthquake measuring 8.0 on the Richter scale in an area where there are no habitations is unlikely to be considered a disaster, although its damage upon the topography may be much greater than a 7.0 magnitude earthquake that strikes an urban area. Even in this case, whether the earthquake is a disaster or not is likely to vary from country to country, or even within a country depending on the level of destruction and loss of human life. Indeed, although it is common to refer to the Richter scale, it is important to stress the limitations of this system. To help take this into account, Japan also uses its own system, the Japan Meteorological Agency Scale (JMS), which measures the intensity of the quake. For a single earthquake, different JMS figures will be produced depending on the intensity of the quake at different locations.

Earthquakes generally lead to a side-to-side shaking, which means that buildings may undergo shear forces, which particularly impacts buildings that are of square or rectangular shapes, as most buildings are. While it is often said that Japanese houses are better adapted to coping with the forces of earthquakes due to the use of wood, such houses also tend to have heavy tiled roofs to help protect against the heavy rain and winds of typhoons. These top-heavy structures tend to topple over during earthquakes. Furthermore, the wooden structures are also a problem should there be a fire. But even seemingly modern buildings can suffer during earthquakes. Another common problem in Japan due to earthquakes is liquefaction, whereby the shaking motion helps to make the water trapped in the ground, particularly prevalent on man-made islands, rise up, which in turn leads to buildings sinking.

Of course, it is not just buildings that suffer from the effects of earthquakes. Perhaps the most well-known images of the Great Hanshin Earthquake in 1995 were the sunken roads due to an underground station beneath collapsing, broken elevated railway lines, the toppled Hanshin Expressway and the sight of a bus dangling over the edge of one piece of collapsed expressway like a scene from *The Italian Job* (Peter Collinson, 1969). The Great Hanshin Earthquake also highlighted a further problem of earthquakes in Japan, in that the streets became littered with falling signs, advertising hoardings, poles and wires. The problem was made all the greater due to the breaking of gas lines, which led to fires being ignited by sparking wires. With water lines being ruptured and roads impassable, fires spread uncontrollably. For us studying Japan, key questions are how this could be allowed to happen, particularly in one of Japan's most affluent cities, and have lessons been learnt?

Rather than the earthquake itself, it was the tsunami that was triggered by the earthquake that caused the greatest damage on 11 March 2011. These phenomena have rarely been filmed and certainly not to the extent that they were on that day. Although some buildings did survive, many did not. Among the buildings to be impacted by the tsunami was the Fukushima Dai-Ichi Nuclear Power Plant. The flooding caused a power outage that ultimately led to a meltdown, explosion and release of radiation into the atmosphere. Work continues to try to bring the site fully under control. While damage was not on the scale of Chernobyl, large areas around the power station are likely to remain uninhabitable for many years. But was the situation avoidable? This is one of the issues we will consider below.

It is common to refer to 'natural disasters' and 'man-made disasters', but there is a problem with the terminology. A natural event itself is not a disaster per se, but whether the society was able to cope with the natural event. As we have discussed elsewhere in the book, we are also seeing increasing urbanisation of the Japanese population, so the potential for a single natural event to become a disaster if it hits one of these areas is seemingly increasing. As with most major accidents and 'man-made disasters', there is often more than one cause, and in some cases the natural forces can also be a contributing factor. However, it is decisions, actions and inactions, or a combination of all of these, that led to the incident taking place. From our perspective as students of Japan, what concerns us is whether there is something about Japanese culture, the way that Japanese organisations operate, or such like, that is helping to 'design' these disasters. This is the issue that we will now focus on.

DEALING WITH DISASTER

Mileti (1999) has referred to disasters being 'designed'. He says that disasters are 'the consequences of narrow and short-sighted development patterns, cultural premises, and attitudes toward both the natural environment and even science and technology' (Mileti 1999: 18). To help us understand some of these issues, please now complete Exercise 8.1.

EXERCISE 8.1

Either think back to the images you have seen on the news about the reporting of the Great East Japan Earthquake or another large scale earthquake in Japan, or watch a summary video of such an event on YouTube. About what proportion of buildings and other infrastructure (e.g. roads and railways) did you see destroyed or damaged due to the direct effects of the earthquake? About what proportion of buildings did you see destroyed or damaged due to subsequent fires or tsunami? During the earthquake, did you see images of people hiding under desks or did they try to continue about their business? Did you see images of people running out into the street? Did you see images of people screaming or otherwise showing emotion?

When a 'high impact, low probability' event strikes, it does not really matter whether the trigger is natural or more 'man-made'; the degree to which this event becomes a disaster or not will be dependent upon the degree to which society is prepared for such an event and how the event is responded to. Japan regularly experiences earthquakes, and so one would expect that Japanese people will not only be relatively accustomed to them, but that when a larger ones strike, they will know what to do. Indeed, on 1 September each year, on the anniversary of the Great Kantō Earthquake in 1923, schools and other institutions will take part in earthquake drills to ensure that people know what to do. Outside of this, it is even possible to go to certain fire stations to get training about what to do during an earthquake and experience what it is like trying to follow some of this training on a special machine that shakes as if in the midst of a major earthquake. But does such training really make a difference? On top of this, the knowledge that Japan will be struck by earthquakes will surely mean that buildings and other structures will be built to the appropriate standards. But is this the case, and if not, why not?

Over the years I have been studying the *shinkansen*, it has been noticeable that the companies have been working to further strengthen the supports for elevated sections. That the Great East Japan Earthquake did not have greater impact on the *shinkansen* may be a sign that these measures were successful. Of course, such measures come at a cost, and there needs to be a system in place that allows for such funding to take place. It is questionable whether such measures would have been possible during the days when JNR was saddled with huge amounts of debt. But while some private companies have been taking the necessary steps to help be prepared for such events, can the same be said more generally?

We have discussed in Chapter 2 the pervasiveness of signs and advertising, and in this chapter about the dangers these posed after the Great Hanshin Earthquake struck Kōbe. While many have also complained about wires for telephones and electricity being unsightly, we also know that they can be dangerous in the wake of an earthquake. So why is more not being done to address these issues? Why has it only been in towns and cities that have been trying to preserve a pre-modernised feel in some districts that significant efforts were made to put as much of the wiring underground as possible? While it may be difficult to widen roads when buildings have already been constructed, to what degree does Japan ever look to build wider roads that may allow for greater emergency access? Even after a major disaster when significant reconstruction will be needed, are new plans developed or do we see largely a rebuilding of what existed before? These are some of the issues that you should be thinking about when doing additional reading about the responses to the Great East Japan Earthquake, for example.

Let us now turn to some of your answers to Exercise 8.1. If you watched clips of the Great East Japan Earthquake, you may well have noticed how there was little sign of damage to buildings due to the earthquake itself, although the intensity in cities such as Sendai was still of a level where, at least historically, much greater levels of damage may have been expected. Of course, what caused the bulk of the devastation that day was the tsunami. Although some buildings did survive, and there are likely to be lessons learnt about how to further improve the design of buildings to withstand tsunami, the greater question is whether the buildings should have been there at all. Stone markers placed throughout history point to spots where previous tsunami had reached and proclaimed that nobody should live or place buildings closer to the coast than these points. Had these lessons from history been heeded, the impact of the tsunami in 2011 would have been much smaller. As we know, the pressures of limited space and 'habitable land', by which we tend to mean land on which it is possible to build rather than it will always be safe to build, is so great in Japan that it seems the marker posts became ignored. Instead, coastal defences were erected in the belief that they would protect the people. They did not. So what is the answer? Build higher walls? Think back to our discussions in Chapter 4 about the use of concrete, and keep in mind both the costs (financial and otherwise) and also who may benefit if taller walls were built. But is it practical for Japan to build huge walls around its coast? How tall would be tall enough? How would this look?

How did Japanese people react during and after the earthquake? Did you see evidence of people getting under desks to protect themselves from falling objects as they are trained to do? Or did you see people standing round looking at TVs, lights and bookcases shaking? Did people stay inside as they are told to do, or did you see examples of people running outside into the street, where they had to dodge falling signs, masonry and glass? For those in coastal areas, did they take the appropriate action to escape any possible tsunami? Of course many did, but sadly there were many more who may not have. Perhaps the problem is the way in which training is done. Are the events on 1 September each year achieving their goals, or are they a form of *tatemae* to provide a degree of reassurance that people know what to do should the unthinkable become a reality? Why not incorporate more training more regularly into people's lives so that there is greater likelihood that people will know what to do? A shining example of how this can be done and how effective it can be was seen in Kamaishi, one of the cities most badly hit by the tsunami, where children learnt in different classes about how to escape from a tsunami (Public Relations Office 2013).

Beyond how people who are caught up in the event are reacting, we also need to consider how other organisations and the government respond to the event. When we do this, we see an alarming number of cases where the government could have done much better. In 1985, it took over 15 hours for the crash site of JAL flight JL123 to be correctly identified. Had it been quicker, it is probable that there would have been more than four survivors found when the search and rescue teams finally reached the site a further five hours later (Hood 2011). In 1995, the governmental responses to the Great Hanshin Earthquake saw a delay in the dispatch and use of the Self Defence Forces, offers of foreign help being rejected or accepted in such a way that the help became less effective and even delays in getting help to people affected by the earthquake. Notoriously, the *Yakuza* were providing more effective aid to the people of Kōbe. The Great Hanshin Earthquake also saw volunteers from across the country offering help in a variety of forms to the extent that 1995 is sometimes referred to as being the first year of voluntary activities in Japan, although this view overlooks the amount of voluntary work that has been done in the past (Hood 2011: 96).

Lessons have been learnt incrementally after each tragedy. Looking at the Great East Japan Earthquake, we see that there is probably still much more the Japanese government could do to improve responses to disasters, particularly in relation to information flow and who takes control. Why had the government not realised before that municipalities might not be able to respond to certain events due to government buildings being destroyed by tsunami? Does the SDF have the equipment needed to respond to flooded areas or to search for people's heat signatures at night? What about the people themselves – what, if anything, will they learn from these disasters? Many Japanese keep a large proportion of their savings in cash in the home. While this may reflect a relative lack of concern about burglaries and a larger concern about banks, as savings in banks will allow them to be stronger and have more money to help with investment, the actions of many Japanese may ordinarily have a negative impact more broadly. However, when houses and savings were lost due to the tsunami after the Great East Japan Earthquake, for many it would have become difficult to prove what had been lost. How does society respond to this? Will behaviour change? Why would we expect behaviour to change? Are Japanese people almost resigning themselves to the fact that major earthquakes, for example, may happen and that they are not going to change their daily behaviour? A 2014 survey found that less than 40 per cent of Tōkyō residents are prepared for a major earthquake (*The Japan Times*, 8 March 2014). With some estimates suggesting that a major earthquake along Japan's Tōkaidō coast could lead to over 300,000 fatalities, perhaps the scale is so great that some either cannot comprehend it or think that in such an event there may be nothing that can be done. Meanwhile, insurance companies are continuing to ramp up the costs for having special coverage for earthquakes (*The Japan Times*, 11 March 2014).

But referring back to Mileti, what is causing Japan to design these disasters? If the SDF do not have the correct equipment, why not? Is it that purchase of equipment is being dictated by the need to maintain good relations with those from whom they are bought rather than being dictated by what may actually be needed? Are the problems of information flow and the time needed to make decisions symptomatic of the processes that we have discussed throughout this book? Does a Japanese management style, whereby people are rotated around jobs every few years to gain experience in a wide range of an organisation's roles, mean that there are not sufficient specialists? Does the culture of *amakudari*, whereby retiring bureaucrats may get jobs in the industry that they have spent their lives working, mean that during their time in the ministry, there may be times when poor safety standards, for example, have not been dealt with due to a fear that such actions may impede the chances of a future career in that company? Or does *amakudari* help to ensure that private companies recruit people who have an in-depth knowledge of the rules and regulations as who may have good connections still within the relevant ministry?

Whatever the answers to these questions, we also have to acknowledge two things. First, there are examples when the Japanese can respond to tragedies, and Japanese teams have regularly been dispatched overseas to help with relief efforts (Hood 2011: 212). Second, we also have to acknowledge that there will still be times where we cannot prepare for every eventuality. The preponderance, perhaps more evident in some cultures than others, that there is always something that can be done is, in my opinion, naive and arrogant in its lack of understanding and respect for the forces of nature in particular. There are times where luck may play a part. It was lucky that JL123 did not crash in an urbanised area. It was lucky that the Great Hanshin Earthquake struck before 06:00, before many were travelling to work. It was lucky that the Great East Japan Earthquake struck in the afternoon and not during the night when people would not have even seen the tsunami coming, let alone have needed more time to awake and respond.

In the longer term after a disaster has occurred, there are many who seem to think that it can be a spur for change. But why? Where are the examples of this happening? There were many great plans for Tōkyō after the Great Kantō Earthquake in 1923, but over time they were scaled back (Schencking 2013). As the American fleet that helped after that quake returned to the US, it stopped at Pearl Harbor where the admiral spoke of the great relations developed between the US and Japan thanks to their assistance and how there was no prospect for war between the two nations within a generation (Schencking 2013: xvi). Standing on the USS Missouri, on which Japan's surrender was signed in 1945, which overlooks the wreck of the USS Arizona in Pearl Harbor, only a few weeks after the Great East Japan Earthquake, I wondered about what other great hopes would be dashed this time.

REPORTING JAPAN

So far, we have been discussing the need to literally build and rebuild Japan, or parts of it, after a disaster. But let us now turn to discussing the building and rebuilding of Japan's image. In this section, we will particularly focus on the building, while the last section will focus on the rebuilding. In terms of building Japan's image, the government may try a number of campaigns, and we cannot overlook the significance of a variety of aspects of Japanese culture and products, let alone the interaction with Japanese people, in how people around the world build their knowledge and own image of what Japan is. However, it is also important to acknowledge the role that the media plays. Television and newspaper reporting are meant to bring a degree of objectivity to the events that are happening, which may not be found in social media, for example. However, can we be confident that what we read about Japan is objective and accurate? Thinking back to our discussion about Barthes' Japan in Chapter 1, there are times when it seems the media should have a disclaimer at the start of all its Japan stories saying this story is written in relation to 'a fictive nation . . . so as to compromise no real country' (Barthes 1983: 3). Although the focus here will be largely on the problems of foreign reporting of Japan, as we shall see, there are times we also have to question the actions of the Japanese media.

If we consider the reporting in relation to the Great East Japan Earthquake, there are a number of issues that are worth noting. On the day of the earthquake itself, many foreign news channels used images from media companies in Japan. However, with no Japanese speaker in the studio, there was nobody to help provide an interpretation or translation of what was being shown. While the lack of linguistic expertise was one problem, the lack of use of people with a knowledge of how Japan operates or understanding of what Japan is like further reduced the capacity for a watching public to comprehend what they were seeing. Perhaps the academic community itself has a responsibility here if people were not willing to help the media organisations, but there also seems to have been a lack of attempt to by the media companies to engage with the experts. During 11 March and the days that followed, the attention began to shift to events at the

Fukushima Dai-Ichi Nuclear Power Station. For those of us following foreign media, Japanese media and social media, it became a tiring business trying to find out what was really happening. Social media has the problem that the reliability of information is sometimes hard to gauge, and that old news can be retweeted and seem current well beyond when it is helpful to the degree that it may actually now be providing incorrect information. Meanwhile, the foreign media were making out the situation in Fukushima to be much worse than most of the Japanese were. Who was right? Why the differences? Was the foreign media assuming that exaggerating the crisis would improve viewing figures or sales? It is said that 'No news is good news', but for media companies perhaps this means that no bad news is no news and so they have come to thrive on negativity. Was the Japanese media trying to keep its consumers calm? Were the Japanese media and those who were interviewed under pressure from others to portray a more positive view? The degree to which either was more accurate in its reporting of Fukushima is beyond the scope of this book. The point it highlights is the need for all of us who study a country to be wary of what we see in the media in relation to Japan. We need to get sufficient understanding of the country and its people ourselves so that we may be able to judge for ourselves the likelihood as to whether a story is accurate or not. The Fukushima case was perhaps extreme, as for those of us concerned with the well-being of students for whom we are responsible that were studying in Japan, we needed accurate information and many of us spent a lot of time developing our knowledge of radiation and such like beyond what any of us had ever probably thought would be necessary. For the most part, the stories that appear in the media will be less critical than this, but one still has to wonder what the impact is of such stories and what the motivations are. Indeed, does it reveal a symptomatic problem with the media that means we cannot rely on the reporting in relation to any foreign country or even our own country? Or is the reporting of Japan unique for some reason?

Let us turn away from the Great East Japan Earthquake and consider some other examples of inaccurate and problematic reporting. If you find an article in a newspaper about the costs of living in Japan, you need to ask whether the journalist is living like a local, and what is the purpose of the story; is it about the cost of Japan or about sending a message to the newspaper itself so that the journalist's expense account does not get cut? In 2013, British newspaper *The Guardian* reported a story about Japanese children needing to wear eyepatches and getting illness due to the popularity of a new craze in eyeball licking. Two months later, a retraction was printed pointing out that the story was completely inaccurate (*The Guardian*, 25 August 2013). So how could the original have been written and printed at all? Is there something different about the world's view of Japan that allows for such stories to be printed? One Japanese academic was so incensed by the nature of an article that appeared in a British newspaper that she commissioned an edited collection where a number of people analysed the article and its weaknesses and what this was representative of (Kondō 2005). Of course, as mentioned above, it is not only foreign media reporting of Japan that we need to be concerned with. For example, the Japanese media made errors in relation to Aum Shinrikyō's first sarin attack in Matsumoto in 1994, which led to the first victims being treated as criminals (see Gamble and Watanabe 2004). That neither the media nor the police did better investigation may itself have had a role in the eventual attack on Tōkyō.

When it comes to the reporting of Japan by foreign media, there seems to be a preponderance to rely on certain clichés and stereotypes and to focus on certain types of story. Is this because most deal with Japan so irregularly that the media feel compelled to include something familiar on to which the rest of the story can be latched? Are the media even going for stories that will help confirm the clichés and stereotypes? Is this why there are seemingly so many articles that revolve around sex, suicide and the portrayal of Japan as different or odd? For many journalists, it would appear that Japan is there to remain exotic and to titillate their readers. To present Japan as normal would not be news-worthy or fit with readers' expectations perhaps. What the media reports, of course, is one of the issues that we have discussed previously as being a problem for all of us when studying Japan. But from our perspective as students of Japan, we need to get beyond the words themselves and question whether what we are seeing is representative, and if it is, what does it actually tell us about Japan? Let us return to the reporting of the aftermath of the Great East Japan Earthquake. In the reports of the behaviour of the Japanese people, one of the most heavily used words was 'stoical'. Were they any more or less stoical than others would be in such a situation? Why is it that the foreign media in China after the Szechuan Earthquake in 2006 focused on those who were accusing authorities of corruption in relation to collapsed buildings, when eyewitnesses I have spoken to have said that most people were sitting around quietly and in shock at what they had seen? And if the Japanese were being particularly 'stoical', is this even as positive as was seemingly being suggested? I wonder what psychologists would say about this apparent suppression of emotion.

But does the reporting of Japan in the media impact your knowledge and image of the country? After all, one of the things that is perhaps most notable about the media's reporting of Japan, at least in the UK for example, is that in most weeks, there will be very few stories about Japan at all. Of course, this lack of reporting means that the problematic stories represent a larger proportion of the total. But if Japan is not being covered much in the media, why not, and does this mean that the media reporting of Japan will not have as great an influence on people as other information sources? Look back to your answers to Exercise 1.1; how many of these items are there because of the media reporting of Japan? Did you even include the Great East Japan Earthquake or any similar event where your knowledge of it was likely to have been defined by the media?

REBUILDING JAPAN ON THE INTERNATIONAL STAGE

In the wake of defeat and its occupation by the Allied Forces, Japan needed to find a way to rebuild itself not only in terms of the buildings and economy, but also its position globally. Something was needed to show the world that Japan was not only back as a major economy, but that it was part of the global community. The answer was the Tōkyō 1964 Olympics. Perhaps it is unsurprising, therefore, that following the Great East Japan Earthquake, Tōkyō's bid to host the 2020 Olympics was also equated to rebuilding the nation's image once more. Just as the *kanji* of the year for 2011 had been *kizuna* due to the events of 11 March (see Chapter 5), so for 2013 it became *rin* (輪, ring) to reflect the successful bid for Tōkyō to host the 2020 Olympics. In this section, let us consider the symbolism of certain events and what their broader impact can be.

The Tōkyō Olympics in 1964 were the first to be held in Asia, and an opportunity to indicate Japan's return to the international stage and the level of modernisation that was taking place in the country. With some events being held in Ōsaka, the world's media was compelled to take the newly opened *shinkansen* and see the results of the huge advances that Japan was making. Even the opening ceremony had a significant piece of symbolism, for rather than using a well-known sportsperson or celebrity to light the flame in the main stadium, in 1964 the flame was lit by Yoshinori Sakai, who had been born on 6 August 1945 in Hiroshima (Horsley and Buckley 1990: 72). The 1964 Tōkyō Olympics were followed up by the 1970 World EXPO held in Ōsaka. This event saw an estimated 62 million Japanese and 2 million foreigners flock to a site to learn more about the world and Japan, as well as be able to enjoy other entertainment (Horsley and Buckley 1990: 108). Since then, Japan has hosted the Winter Olympics in 1972 (Sapporo) and 1998 (Nagano), been co-host of the Football World Cup in 2002 and has hosted another EXPO (2005, Aichi prefecture). Japan has also been host to a variety of other major international events. Japan will also host the Rugby World Cup in 2019, although no Japanese team, which has *sakura* as its badge, has ever won a single match at previous World Cups. With Japan already backing a bid for the 2020 Summer Olympics, it was hardly a surprise that the bid became so linked to efforts to revitalise the country's spirits and desire to rebuild in the aftermath of the Great East Japan Earthquake. Indeed, this is the message that Prime Minister Abe took with him when he flew on the government's jumbo jet to the meeting where the winning bid would be announced (see Figure 8.1).

Let us look at what the impact of Tōkyō hosting the 2020 Olympics may have. These are issues that you should continue to monitor and consider as you watch the events themselves in due course. The Olympics will require a lot of construction work to

Figure 8.1 Rebuilding Japan. The government's Jumbo Jet prepares to depart Haneda Airport to take PM Abe to meetings including the one to decide the host city for the 2020 Olympics. Haneda Airport, and the multitude of companies that serve it, will be looking to benefit from Tōkyō's successful bid. In the background, about 18km away, Tōkyō Sky Tree, another symbol of Japan's continuing modernisation and advancements towers over the skyline.

be conducted not only for the stadia and other facilities directly connected to the event, but also in terms of infrastructure (airport expansion, road and rail improvements) and hotels, for example. Of course, while this will have a short-term benefit for many, one has to remember that there are likely to be those who will not benefit as they have to move their home or business (e.g. Japan Today, 6 September 2013), and some businesses see others get a boost from contracts that they were unable to get, and such like.

Indeed, some have even suggested that the only certain winners from the construction plans are the *Yakuza* (*The Japan Times*, 15 February 2014). In the long run, will the 'improvements' continue to help, or will overcapacity lead to additional costs and problems?

Although hosting the Olympics should have a positive economic impact, for some there are questions about how widely it will be felt. In particular, given the link between the event and the Great East Japan Earthquake, one has to wonder what, if any, positive impact there will be on the Tōhoku region, which was most badly affected by the earthquake and tsunami. But let us think beyond the economic and think about what the Olympics could do in relation to further improving the image and knowledge of Japan around the world. For example, it would be nice to think that perhaps now foreign commentators will give more attention to how to pronounce Japanese names and words correctly, although there have been opportunities to do this in the past so there is no reason to think that things may be any different this time. Indeed, language issues are one of the concerns that the organisers are looking to address. While it is possible to survive in most countries without a knowledge of the local language, and technology may be making this even more the case, Tōkyō is looking to improve the number of multilingual signs, for example (*The Japan Times*, 19 March 2014). Of course, we need to consider where the visitors are likely to come from in terms of what languages should appear on signs. Figure 8.2 shows the nationality of foreign visitors to Japan in recent years. We can see from this that despite the political disputes that may occur, there are still huge numbers of visitors from China and South Korea, for example. Although the total passed 10 million for the first time ever in 2013, this is still short of the target of 30 million per year by 2030 (*The Japan Times*, 20 December 2013).

Will further increases in international visitors help with an internationalisation of Japan more broadly? We have previously discussed some of the problems associated with nationalism within Japan and how this may even be an impediment to further immigration. Is Tōkyō 2020 an opportunity to address this? Or will the interests of some parts of the government, which may wish to see low levels of immigration due to a perception that increases would lead to increased crime levels, mean that changes will be largely superficial? Multilingual signs may help to remind

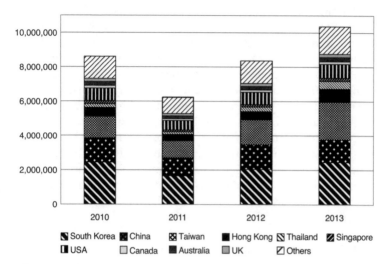

Figure 8.2 Foreign visitors to Japan

Source: Figure by the author based on Ministry of Internal Affairs and Communications (2013: 105) and JNTO (2014).

Japanese people that not all foreigners are '*eigo no hito*', or an English-speaking person, as I have been referred to once by a child who was clearly trying to avoid saying *gaijin* or even *gaikokujin*. But of course the reality is that English has become a language studied by many as a foreign language as is frequently used by people for whom none it is their native language. While there may be some who consider *gaijin* to be derogatory, as it has the meaning of 'alien', such a view probably overlooks the origins of the word foreigner, which they may equate with *gaikokujin*, and that it has nothing to do with ET, for example. What is more puzzling is perhaps why some Japanese people continue to call non-Japanese *gaijin* or *gaikokujin* even when they are visiting another country. Just as the 1964 Olympics were used as a mechanism to improve the driving standards of the infamous *kamikaze* taxi drivers (Horisaka 2013), perhaps the 2020 Olympics can be the means to further truly internationalise Japan.

If more do go to Japan as a result of Tōkyō 2020, what will they see and experience? What will they take back to their own countries from Japan from these sights and experiences? Will they understand everything that they see around them? Will visits be limited to key sights in Tōkyō, Mount Fuji and Kyōto, or will people venture around more? What will it take for the Daisen Kofun (Chapter 6) to become more widely known? Will more explore to see sights such as the night view of Hakodate (see Figure 8.3)? Or does the abundance of spectacular sights across Japan hold some Japanese back from travelling overseas? A trip by train alongside the Kiso River will mean that you get commentary saying that this is the Japanese Rhein. Does being the Japanese Rhein mean that visitors to the River Kiso feel that a domestic trip rather than a foreign one is sufficient? You will then arrive in the Japan Alps, so named due to their resemblance of their European counterpart. So is there any need to travel to the (European) Alps?

However, the expansion of the airports for hosting Tōkyō 2020 and the greater provision of cheap air travel to nearby nations (see Chapter 3) means there are greater opportunities for Japanese to travel overseas. Figure 8.4 shows the numbers and destinations for Japanese visitors. Compare this with Figure 8.2 and you can

Figure 8.3 The night view of Hakodate. The spectacular night view across Hakodate is ranked as one of the best views in Japan, together with Kōbe and Nagasaki, and as one of the best night views in the world alongside Hong Kong and Napoli according to Michelin.

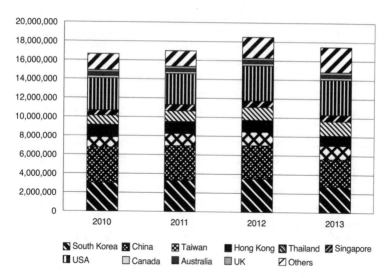

South Korea ☒ China ☒ Taiwan ■ Hong Kong ☒ Thailand ☒ Singapore
■ USA □ Canada ■ Australia □ UK ☑ Others

Figure 8.4 Japanese visits overseas

Source: Figure by the author based on Japan Tourism Marketing Co. (2014). No data available for Singapore in 2012 and 2013 or for USA in 2013 or UK in 2013, so estimates have been used.

see that there are some notable imbalances. First, there are nearly double the number of Japanese going overseas than are going to Japan. However, what the figure does not show is the number of nights' stay the trips are. Many Japanese will only go overseas for a few days, whereas visitors to Japan may stay for at least a week. In terms of location, we see that there are significantly more Japanese visitors to the USA than are coming from the USA. About 40 per cent of the visits to the USA are to Hawai'i alone. Within the others, around 900,000 Japanese are also travelling to Guam each year. In Europe, France and Germany also see significantly higher numbers of visitors from Japan than the UK.

What Figure 8.4 also does not show is the change in type of person going overseas from Japan. For example, there appear to be less Japanese university students going overseas (MEXT 2012). While changes in exchange rates may play a larger role due to the extended period abroad, there are other things that may be playing a part. For example, changes to the time when university students start job-hunting may be impacting the numbers who take part in exchange programmes. A few isolated cases of crimes or terrorism in some countries appear to have put off some from travelling overseas, regardless of whether such things are possible in Japan too.

While the focus has largely been on what can be done domestically to encourage people to come to Japan, what may still need further attention is how to boost international engagement. Putting up multilingual signs is meaningless if visitors who do want to interact with Japanese people find it difficult to do so as Japanese people do not have sufficient linguistic abilities to do so. There is no point in concerning ourselves with whether non-Japanese pronounce Japanese names and words correctly if more Japanese people do not put more effort into pronouncing and spelling names of other languages correctly. Japan cannot expect the world to buy Japanese products if it shifts to a more isolationist stance. A number of initiatives have been tried over the years to try to improve the quality of English-language tuition in Japan in particular, but most have seemingly had limited impact. Is this because the style of examinations, which are often multiple-choice, does not lend itself to proper development of linguistic skills? Is it that the focus has been on trying to help the students rather than the teachers, who often are not specialists in foreign languages? Does the emphasis on credentials and lack of confidence to test actual ability of an individual mean that skilled people are being put off from jobs where they can use their language skills?

Returning to the Tōkyō 2020 Olympics, another measure by which some will judge its success in rebuilding Japan relates to how Japan performs at the Olympics themselves. For many Japanese, the 1964 Olympics will always be remembered as the Olympics of the women's volleyball team. The gold medal performance was not only one of the most watched programmes ever in Japan, but it also helped to raise an awareness of issues relating to women's place in society (Macnaughtan 2014). In recent years, it has been women's football that has been the source of much of Japan's success on the international stage. With concerns about the levels of fitness of the public and children generally, Tōkyō 2020 may be used as a spur to try to encourage more into sports. Will this lead to more success? What will be the limitations to this? How can it be achieved? These are just some of the questions that Japan itself is now battling with.

SUMMARY

This chapter has addressed how Japan responds to major incidents. While this chapter has focused particularly on earthquakes and their impact, we should not overlook the other natural forces that Japan has to contend with. Other chapters have mentioned the challenges from the weather. On top of this, Japan also has a number of active volcanoes. Even Mount Fuji may erupt again one day. While this has the potential to cause much damage to the surrounding area, given the broader discussion in this chapter and throughout the book you may want to give some thought about what the symbolic and wider impact of such an eruption of one of Japan's main icons would be. While Japan has continued to rebuild areas impacted by the Great East Japan Earthquake, there is much still to be done, and this chapter has raised issues with the way in which it and other major incidents have been handled and what lessons can be learnt from this. The chapter has also highlighted that the reporting in the media of such events, as well as other stories, may be distorting our understanding of the country and its people. Finally, the chapter looked at how the Tōkyō 2020 Olympics have become entwined with the effort to not only rebuild Japan economically, but also (re)build its image on the international stage.

9

CONCLUSIONS

Understanding any country is not an easy process. There is no quick fix. It requires time and research. Studying Japan is like putting together the pieces of a jigsaw puzzle. This book has used a number of images and symbols of Japan to help us understand Japan more widely. We have taken these images and pulled them apart to see what is relevant about them, what clues there are about the country itself in the pictures and so on. We have seen how many different issues relate to others, hence the number of cross-references to other chapters throughout the book. It is only by putting the pieces together that one can start to get a complete picture. Unlike a jigsaw puzzle, however, you may never have all the pieces and be sure when you have the complete picture, so you have to keep looking, researching and wanting to learn more.

In this book, we have taken examples of stories that are presented in the news, how Japan is portrayed in movies and the diverse forms of Japan's exports, and by treating them as 'symbols' use them as the basis on which aspects of Japan, its society and culture can be explored, discussed and studied. I have deliberately tried to limit the number of symbols that I have discussed and analysed – certain ones (Mount Fuji, the *shinkansen* and sights around Shibuya) have come up in numerous chapters. This is not because they are more significant, but rather I wanted to demonstrate just how many diverse aspects of Japan can be discussed using limited symbols. I also have not discussed these symbols in their entirety – there is still much you can do with them. On top of this, I hope that you will be encouraged to study Japan through other symbols that I have not used. In particular, I have deliberately not included much discussion about *manga* and *anime*, which has become an interest of many of those studying Japan, as I am keen to encourage those with such interests to think about how to use their interest in this subject to study Japan more broadly. The themes within this book should have provided you with the framework by which you can do this.

I hope that this book has inspired you to learn more about Japan. I also hope that it has inspired you to learn Japanese. Although, as we discussed in Chapter 1, knowing the language is not always a necessity, it can certainly help. There are situations where using Japanese is likely to help you get the result you are looking for more easily than speaking English, for example. But if you are going to learn the language, I would like to offer one piece of advice – focus on things that interest you rather than going for hunting for things that are 'typically Japanese'. While learning the vocabulary related to the tea ceremony and learning the tea ceremony will help you learn something of the language and culture, if this is not the sort of activity that is going to keep your motivation for learning about Japan and its language fired up, then perhaps it is not what you should be focusing upon. As we have seen in the discussions in this book, even seemingly 'foreign' things can teach us much about Japan. So if your interests are a particular sport or hobby, for example, try to find Japanese materials related to them.

By the same token, and as we have also discussed in the book, what do we even mean by something being Japanese? Take, for example, the symbol that appears on the book cover itself. It has been suggested that one of the symbols of Japan, cherry blossom (*sakura*), may actually originate in South Korea (*The Japan Times*, 20 March 2014b). Does this matter? After all, the trees date back to before there were countries and possibly even humans. *Sakura* can be found in many countries today, but the nature of the meanings, emotions and festivities that are connected with it vary greatly. As students of Japan, we need to understand and respect the different interpretations that can exist depending on the context and where we are.

When you visit Japan, study everything. I used to go to France as a child, but as the holidays were largely beach holidays I could hardly claim that I had seen much of what real French life was like. You need to get in and try to live as the locals live. As you do so, look at everything, but do not go hunting for the differences between Japan and your own country. Try to understand what you are seeing. Then try to find studies that will help to explain the issues. Even if you ask a Japanese person to provide an explanation, can you be sure that he or she knows the correct answer? How certain could you be that you would be able to provide an accurate answer if you were asked a similar question about your country? Remember, there may be more than one interpretation, so do not necessarily settle for the first one that you come to. Things can also change over time.

Throughout this book, I have asked you to do a number of exercises. There has been at least one for each chapter. What of the exercise for this chapter? Look back to your symbols written down as part of Exercise 1.1. How will you use these symbols to study Japan? But do not just use this list. You need to add to it as you continue your studies of Japan, as otherwise all you will be destined to do is study many of the same symbols that have been passed down to us over the years. This is the exercise to which you must now turn.

BIBLIOGRAPHY

Airline Leader (2013) 'World routes special report', available at: www.airlineleader.com/this-months-highlights/world-routes-special-report (accessed 15 September 2013).

Anime News Network (2008) 'Hello Kitty named Japan's tourism ambassador to China', available at: www.animenewsnetwork.co.uk/news/2008-05-19/hello-kitty-named-japan-tourism-ambassador-to-china (accessed 25 May 2008).

anna.aero (2013) 'Japanese domestic air travel market growing again thanks to emergence of AirAsia Japan, Jetstar Japan and Peach', available at: www.anna.aero/2013/03/27/japanese-domestic-air-travel-market-growing-again-thanks-to-emergence-of-airasia-japan-jetstar-japan-and-peach/ (accessed 28 March 2013).

area-info (2014a) 'Ueno-mura', available at: http://area-info.jpn.org/area103667.html (accessed 4 April 2014).

area-info (2014b) 'Komoro', available at: http://area-info.jpn.org/area202088.html (accessed 4 April 2014).

area-info (2014c) 'Iiyama', available at: http://area-info.jpn.org/area202134.html (accessed 4 April 2014).

Barthes, R. (1983) *Empire of Signs*, New York: Hill & Wang.

Bauer, J. R. (2006) *Forging Environmentalism*, New York: M. E. Sharpe.

BBC (27 June 2003) 'Fury over Japan rape gaffe', available at: http://news.bbc.co.uk/1/hi/world/asia-pacific/3025240.stm (accessed 27 June 2003).

BBC (10 February 2010) 'Toyota bows and the Japanese art of apology', available at: http://news.bbc.co.uk/1/hi/world/asia-pacific/8508531.stm (accessed 10 February 2010).

BBC (21 January 2013) 'Dreamliner: Japan and US probe battery maker', available at: www.bbc.co.uk/news/business-21115383 (accessed 21 January 2013).

BBC (22 January 2014) 'Japan's ANA pulls "racist" advert', available at: www.bbc.co.uk/news/business-25838396 (accessed 22 January 2014).

BP (2014) 'Historical data workbook: crude oil prices 1861–2012', available at: www.bp.com/en/global/corporate/about-bp/energy-economics/statistical-review-of-world-energy-2013.html (accessed 2 April 2014).

Bureau of Labor Statistics (2012) 'Focus on prices and spending', available at: www.bls.gov/opub/focus/volume2_number16/cex_2_16.htm (accessed 1 October 2013).

Buruma, I. (2001) *A Japanese Mirror: Heroes and Villains in Japanese Culture*, London: Phoenix (original edition 1984).

Cabinet Office (2010) '*Hakkenchi to sumaichi hikakuhyō (shikuchōsonbetsu)*', available at: www8.cao.go.jp/jisatsutaisaku/kyouka_basic_data/h21/pdf/4-1-3.pdf (accessed 12 December 2011).

Cabinet Office (2014) '*Tōhoku Chihō Taiheiyōoki Jishin (Higashi Nihon Daishinsai) Nitsuite*', available at: www.kantei.go.jp/saigai/pdf/201403131700jisin.pdf (accessed 7 April 2014).

Cave, P. (2007) *Primary School in Japan: Self, Individuality and Learning in Elementary Education*, London: Routledge.

Chandler, D. (2007) *Semiotics: The Basics*, 2nd edition, Abingdon: Routledge.

Cohen, A. (1986) *Symbolising Boundaries: Identity and Diversity in British Cultures*, Manchester: Manchester University Press.

Condon, J. (1991) *A Half Step Behind*, Rutland: Charles Tuttle.

The Daily Telegraph (5 November 2000) 'Japan struggles with soaring death toll in Suicide Forest'.

The Daily Telegraph (4 May 2009) 'Japanese suicides rise as world recession hits country's businessmen'.

Dentsū (2013) 'Advertising expenditures in Japan', available at: www.dentsu.com/books/pdf/expenditures_2012.pdf (accessed 3 July 2013).

Duke, B. (1986) *The Japanese School: Lessons for Industrial America*, New York: Praeger.

Dusinberre, M. (2012) *Hard Times in the Hometown*, Honolulu, HI: University of Hawai'i Press.

Forbes (2014) 'Company information', available at: www.forbes.com/companies/ (accessed 7 April 2014).

Fujita, K. and Hill, R. C. (2005) *Innovative Tokyo*, Washington, DC: World Bank Publications.

Fujiwara, C. (2008) 'Single mothers and welfare restructuring in Japan: gender and class dimensions of income and employment', available at: http://japanfocus.org/-Fujiwara-Chisa/2623 (accessed 12 October 2013).

Fukushima, M. (2014) '*Fukushima Mizuho no dokidoki nikki*', available at: http://mizuhofukushima.blog83.fc2.com/blog-entry-2436.html (accessed 10 February 2014).

FX Top (2014) 'Historical comparison', available at: http://fxtop.com/en/historical-exchange-rates-comparison.php (accessed 2 April 2014).

Galbraith, P. W. and Karlin, J. G. (eds) (2012) *Idols and Celebrity in Japanese Media Culture*, Basingstoke: Palgrave Macmillan.

Gamble, A. and Watanabe, T. (2004) *A Public Betrayed: Japanese Media Atrocities, What the World Needs to Know*, Washington, DC: Regnery.

Greater London Authority (2014) 'Population of London', available at: http://data.london.gov.uk/datastore/population-london (accessed 2 April 2014).

Goodman, R., Imoto, Y. and Toivonen, T. (eds) (2012) *A Sociology of Japanese Youth: From Returnees to NEETs*, London: Routledge.

Groth, D. (1996) 'Media and political protest: the bullet train movements', in S. J. Pharr and E. S. Krauss (eds), *Media and Politics in Japan*, Honolulu, HI: University of Hawai'i Press, pp. 213–41.

The Guardian (23 January 2011) 'BBC apologizes for Japanese atomic bomb jokes on QI quiz show', available at: www.theguardian.com/media/2011/jan/23/bbc-apology-atomic-bomb-jokes (accessed 24 January 2011).

The Guardian (25 August 2013) 'The readers' editor on . . . how we fell into the trap of reporting Japan's eyeball-licking craze as fact', available at: www.theguardian.com/commentisfree/2013/aug/25/guardian-japan-eyeball-licking-craze-hoax (accessed 25 August 2013).

Hearn, L. (2005) *Glimpses of Unfamiliar Japan*, Public Domain Books, Kindle Edition (original edition 1894).

Heinze, U. (2011) 'Radio and television consumption in Japan', *Electronic Journal of Contemporary Japanese Studies*, available at: www.japanesestudies.org.uk/articles/2011/Heinze.html (accessed 15 September 2013).

Hendry, J. (1995) *Wrapping Culture: Politeness, Presentation and Power in Japan and Other Societies*, Oxford: Clarendon Press.

Hendry, J. (1999) *Other People's Worlds*, New York: New York University Press.

Hendry, J. (2012) *Understanding Japanese Society*, London: Routledge.

Hood, C. P. (2001) *Education Reform in Japan: Nakasone's Legacy*, London: Routledge.

Hood, C. P. (2006a) Shinkansen*: From Bullet Train to Symbol of Modern Japan*, London: Routledge.

Hood, C. P. (2006b) 'From polling station to political station? Politics and the *Shinkansen*', *Japan Forum*, 18(1): 45–63.

Hood, C. P. (2011) *Dealing with Disaster in Japan: Responses to the Flight JL123 Crash*, London: Routledge.

Hood, C. P. (2012) 'Disaster and death in Japan: responses to the Flight JL123 crash', in H. Suzuki (ed.), *Death and Dying in Contemporary Japan: Shifting Social Structures and Values*, London: Routledge, pp. 202–25.

Horisaka, K. (2013) 'A shockwave from the Mecca of soccer, Brazil', *AJISS Commentary*, available at: www2.jiia.or.jp/en_commentary/201308/21-1.html (accessed 22 August 2013).

Horsley, W. and Buckley, R. (1990) *Nippon: New Superpower*, London: BBC Books.

The Independent (17 January 2014) 'Hiroo Onoda, the last Japanese soldier to give himself in: "When I surrendered, the past seemed like a dream"', available at: www.independent.co.uk/news/world/asia/hiroo-onoda-the-last-japanese-soldier-to-give-himself-in-when-i-surrendered-the-past-seemed-like-a-dream-9068009.html (accessed 17 January 2014).

Institute for Global Environmental Strategies (2013) 'The rebirth of the "Sea of Death": history of the recovery of Dokai Bay', available at: http://pub.iges.or.jp/contents/76/eng/story/storyi2.htm (accessed 2 September 2013).

Isomae, J. (2013) 'Discursive formations surrounding "religious freedom" in modern Japan: religion, Shintō, the emperor institution', in L. Hölscher and M. Eggert (eds), *Religion and Secularity*, Leiden: Brill.

IWC (2014a) 'Whale population estimates', available at: http://iwc.int/estimate (accessed 4 April 2014).

IWC (2014b) 'Aboriginal subsistence whaling', available at: http://iwc.int/aboriginal (accessed 4 April 2014).

Jansen, M. B. (2009) *The Making of Modern Japan*, Cambridge, MA: Harvard University Press.

Japan Market Resource Network (JMRN) (2007) 'Japan's changing consumer', available at: www.jmrn.com/UserFiles/File/DCLB_JMRN.pdf (accessed 14 October 2013).

The Japan Times (20 October 2009) 'Abortion still key birth control', available at: www.japantimes.co.jp/news/2009/10/20/reference/abortion-still-key-birth-control/#.UzyBOfldXiU (accessed 21 October 2009).

The Japan Times (27 May 2011) 'Kan sets 20% target for renewable energy', available at: www.japantimes.co.jp/news/2011/05/27/national/kan-sets-20-target-for-renewable-energy/#.Uz7DO_ldXiU (accessed 27 May 2011).

The Japan Times (26 June 2011) 'Exploring the Sea of Trees' fatal attraction'.

The Japan Times (20 April 2013) 'Doraemon trumps Hello Kitty for Olympic Games ambassador', available at: www.japantimes.co.jp/community/2013/04/20/our-lives/doraemon-trumps-hello-kitty-for-olympic-games-ambassador/#.U0MJP_ldXiU (accessed 20 April 2013).

The Japan Times (15 August 2013) 'Female managers are still rare in most firms, survey finds', available at: www.japantimes.co.jp/news/2013/08/15/business/female-managers-still-rare-in-most-firms-survey-finds/#.UzxxCvldXiU (accessed 16 August 2013).

The Japan Times (23 September 2013) '*Matahara*: turning the clock back on women's rights', available at: www.japantimes.co.jp/community/2013/09/

23/issues/matahara-turning-the-clock-back-on-womens-rights/#.UzxwF_ldXiW (accessed 24 September 2013).

The Japan Times (20 December 2013) 'Japan achieves 10 million tourists for 2013', available at: www.japantimes.co.jp/news/2013/12/20/national/japan-achieves-10-million-tourist-target-for-2013/#.U0RnCvldXiU (accessed 20 December 2013).

The Japan Times (15 February 2014) 'Sure winners in 2020 Tokyo Olympics? Gangsters', available at: www.japantimes.co.jp/news/2014/02/15/business/sure-winners-in-2020-tokyo-olympics-gangsters/ (accessed 15 February 2014).

The Japan Times (5 March 2014) 'Yamagata *Shinkansen* to get foot baths, tatami', available at: www.japantimes.co.jp/news/2014/03/05/national/yamagata-bullet-train-to-get-foot-baths-tatami/ (accessed 5 March 2014).

The Japan Times (8 March 2014) 'Fewer than 40 percent of Tokyoites prepared for big quake', available at: www.japantimes.co.jp/news/2014/03/08/national/fewer-than-40-percent-of-tokyoites-prepared-for-big-quake/ (accessed 8 March 2014).

The Japan Times (11 March 2014) 'Quake coverage to cost 15.5% more', available at: www.japantimes.co.jp/news/2014/03/11/business/quake-coverage-to-cost-15-5-more/#.U0RR7vldXiU (accessed 11 March 2014).

The Japan Times (19 March 2014) 'Tokyo to put up more multi-language signs for Olympics', available at: www.japantimes.co.jp/news/2014/03/19/national/tokyo-to-put-up-more-multi-language-signs-for-olympics/ (accessed 19 March 2014).

The Japan Times (20 March 2014a) 'Giant robots officially fly the flag for cool Japan', available at: www.japantimes.co.jp/life/2014/03/20/lifestyle/giant-robots-officially-fly-the-flag-for-cool-japan/#.U0YkSfldXiU (accessed 20 March 2014).

The Japan Times (20 March 2014b) 'Did Japan's hallowed cherry trees actually originate in South Korea?', available at: www.japantimes.co.jp/news/2014/03/20/national/did-japans-hallowed-cherry-trees-actually-originate-in-south-korea/#.U0TaW_ldXiU (accessed 20 March 2014).

Japan Today (6 September 2013) '2020 Olympics may spell end for Shinjuku's "Golden Gai"', available at: www.japantoday.com/category/kuchikomi/view/2020-olympics-might-spell-end-for-shinjukus-golden-gai (accessed 15 September 2013).

Japan Today (26 September 2013) '1 in 3 Japanese women want to be housewives: poll', available at: www.japantoday.com/category/national/view/1-in-3-japanese-women-want-to-be-housewives-poll (accessed 26 September 2013).

Japan Today (26 December 2013) 'Mt Fuji climbing fee set at Y1000', available at: www.japantoday.com/category/national/view/mt-fuji-climbing-fee-set-at-y1000 (accessed 26 December 2013).

Japan Today (9 February 2014) 'Who owns Mt Fuji? The answer will probably surprise (and confuse) you', available at: www.japantoday.com/category/arts-culture/view/who-owns-mt-fuji-the-answer-will-probably-surprise-and-confuse-you (accessed 9 February 2014).

Japan Today (26 February 2014) 'Blessing for a blast-off', available at: www.japantoday.com/category/picture-of-the-day/view/blessing-for-a-blast-off (accessed 26 February 2014).

Japan Today (30 March 2014) 'Biggest threat to Japan whaling: declining appetites', available at: www.japantoday.com/category/national/view/biggest-threat-to-japan-whaling-declining-appetites (accessed 30 March 2014).

Japan Tourism Marketing Co. (2014) 'Historical statistics – Japanese tourists travelling abroad', available at: www.tourism.jp/en/statistics/outbound/ (accessed 9 April 2014).

JNTO (2014) '2013 foreign visitors', available at: www.jnto.go.jp/eng/ttp/sta/PDF/E2013.pdf (accessed 8 April 2014).

JR East (2014) 'Yamagata Shinkansen-ni Atarana Miryoku-ga Tanjō Shimasu!', available at: www.jreast.co.jp/press/2013/20140303.pdf (accessed 5 March 2014).

JR Tōkai (2013) Data Book 2013, Tōkyō: Central Japan Railway Company.

Japan Wind Power Association (JWPA) (2014) 'JWPA report detail', available at: http://jwpa.jp/page_189_englishsite/jwpa/detail_e.html (accessed 14 February 2014).

Kajii, M. (1924) Remon, Tōkyō: Kadokawa Shoten.

Kasai, Y. (2003) Japanese National Railways – Its Break-up and Privatization, Folkestone: Global Oriental.

Kingston, J. (2012) Contemporary Japan, Chichester: John Wiley & Sons.

Kinmonth, E. (2014) 'Corporate culture', email to NBR's Japan Forum mailing list, 9 April 2014.

Kinsella, S. (2000) Adult Manga: Culture and Power in Contemporary Japanese Society, Honolulu, HI: University of Hawai'i Press.

Kirsch, G. (2014) 'Bringing the past to the present: Japanese television and public memories of the Pacific War', Cardiff Japanese Studies Seminar, Cardiff University, 6 February 2014.

Kondō, K. (ed.) (2005) Yuganda Kagami-ni Utsutta Nihon – Japan Reflected in a Cracked Mirror, Tokyo: GNAC.

Krauss, E. (2000) Broadcasting Politics in Japan: NHK and Television News, Ithaca, NY: Cornell University Press.

Littlewood, I. (1996) The Idea of Japan: Western Images, Western Myths, London: Secker & Warburg.

Macnaughtan, H. (2014) 'The oriental witches: women, volleyball and the 1964 Tokyo Olympics', Sport in History, 34(1): 134–56.

Matanle, P. (2011) 'The historical arc of regional shrinkage in Japan', in P. Matanle and A. S. Rausch (eds), *Japan's Shrinking Regions*, Amherst, NY: Cambria Press, pp. 83–132.

Melville, H. (1851) *Moby Dick, or the Whale*, New York: Harper & Brothers.

Metcalf, P. (2005) *Anthropology: The Basics*, Abingdon: Routledge.

Mileti, D. (1999) *Disasters by Design: A Reassessment of Natural Hazards in the United States*, Washington, DC: Joseph Henry Press.

Minami-Satsuma-shi (2013) '*Tsuwachan Takushī Akime Riyōannai*', available at: www.city.minamisatsuma.lg.jp/%E3%81%A4%E3%82%8F%E3%81%A1%E3%82%83%E3%82%93%E3%82%BF%E3%82%AF%E3%82%B7%E3%83%BC%E7%A7%8B%E7%9B%AE%E7%B7%9A%E5%88%A9%E7%94%A8%E6%A1%88%E5%86%85.pdf (accessed 10 August 2013).

Meyer, G. (2007) Commentary on DVD for 'Thirty Minutes of Tokyo', *The Simpsons: The Complete 10th Season*, 20th Century Fox.

Ministry of Education, Culture, Sports, Science and Technology (MEXT) (2006) 'Basic Act on Education', available at: www.mext.go.jp/english/law andplan/1303462.htm (accessed 1 May 2007).

Ministry of Education, Culture, Sports, Science and Technology (MEXT) (2012) 'On the number of Japanese studying abroad', available at: www.mext.go.jp/english/topics/__icsFiles/afieldfile/2012/02/17/1316751_1.pdf (accessed 9 April 2014).

Ministry of the Environment (2013) '*Heisei 25nen Kaki no Fujisan Tozanshasū nit suite*', available at: http://kanto.env.go.jp/pre_2013/0910a.html (accessed 25 September 2013).

Ministry of Finance (2013) 'Highlights of the Budget for FY2013', available at: www.mof.go.jp/english/budget/budget/fy2013/01.pdf (accessed 3 July 2013).

Ministry of Health, Labour and Welfare (2014) '*Todōfukenbetsu ni mita gōkei tokushu shusseiritsu no nenjisuī*', available at: www.mhlw.go.jp/toukei/saikin/hw/jinkou/suii09/brth4.html (accessed 15 January 2014).

Ministry of Internal Affairs and Communications (2010) '*Heisei no Gappei ni yoru Shichōsonsū no henka*', available at: www.soumu.go.jp/gapei/pdf/090416_09.pdf (accessed 15 May 2013).

Ministry of Internal Affairs and Communications (2013) *Statistical Handbook of Japan 2013*, Statistics Bureau, Ministry of Internal Affairs and Communications.

Ministry of Internal Affairs and Communications (2014) 'Religious organisations, clergymen and adherents', available at: www.stat.go.jp/data/nenkan/zuhyou/y2322a00.xls (accessed 14 January 2014).

Ministry of Land, Infrastructure, Transport and Tourism (MLIT) (2014) 'Average prices of building land by use and prefecture (2012)', available at: www.stat.go.jp/english/data/nenkan/1431-17.htm (accessed 3 April 2014).

Mito, Y. (2002) *Teikoku Hassha*, Tōkyō: Kōtsū Shimbunsha.

NBC (2009) 'World reaction, page 21', available at: www.nbcnews.com/id/28753038/displaymode/1107/s/2/framenumber/21/ (accessed 21 January 2009).

NBR Forum (2014) 'Another defeat for Japanese IT industries', post to discussion group by Minoru Mochizuki using data from VLSI Research, 27 February 2014.

Nenji-toukei (2014a) '*100-sai ijō kōreisha sū*', available at: http://nenji-toukei.com/n/kiji/10030/100%E6%AD%B3%E4%BB%A5%E4%B8%8A%E9%AB%98%E9%BD%A2%E8%80%85%E6%95%B0 (accessed 3 April 2014).

Nenji-toukei (2014b) '*Jisatsushasū*', available at: http://nenji-toukei.com/n/kiji/10043/%E8%87%AA%E6%AE%BA%E8%80%85%E6%95%B0 (accessed 5 April 2014).

New York City (2014) 'Population', available at: www.nyc.gov/html/dcp/html/census/popcur.shtml (accessed 2 April 2014).

New York Times, 23 August 2013, 'Japan's women to the rescue', available at: http://economix.blogs.nytimes.com/2013/08/23/japans-women-to-the-rescue/?_php=true&_type=blogs&_php=true&_type=blogs&_r=1 (accessed 24 August 2013).

News on Japan (6 September 2013) 'Filming curtailed in "suicide forest"', available at: www.newsonjapan.com/html/newsdesk/article/98171.php (accessed 6 September 2013).

Nikkei (2014) 'Newspapers in Japan', http://adweb.nikkei.co.jp/english/newspapers_in_japan/ (accessed 2 April 2014).

Noguchi, T. and Fujii, T. (2000) 'Minimizing the effect of natural disasters', *Japan Railway & Transport Review*, 23: 52–9.

OECD (2011) 'Suicide mortality rates, 2009', available at: http://dx.doi.org/10.1787/888932523557 (accessed 1 December 2011).

OECD (2013) 'Household saving rates', available at: www.oecd-ilibrary.org/content/table/2074384x-table7 (accessed 4 July 2013).

OECD (2014) 'Total fertility rates', available at: www.oecd-ilibrary.org/sites/factbook-2011-en/02/01/01/index.html;jsessionid=9formejhi1sdj.delta?contentType=/ns/StatisticalPublication,/ns/Chapter&itemId=/content/chapter/factbook-2011-9-en&containerItemId=/content/serial/18147364&accessItemIds=&mimeType=text/html (accessed 15 January 2014).

Okimoto, D. (1989) *Between MITI and the Market: Japanese Industrial Policy for High Technology*, Palo Alto, CA: Stanford University Press.

Olcott, G. (2009) *Conflict and Change*, Cambridge: Cambridge University Press.

Ollhoff, J. (2010) *Samurai*, Edina: ABDO.

Onoda, H. (2013) *No Surrender: My Thirty-Year War*, Tōkyō: Kōdansha.

Palin, M. (1997) *Full Circle*, London: BBC.

Public Relations Office (2013) 'The miracle of Kamaishi', available at: http://mnj.gov-online.go.jp/kamaishi.html (accessed 1 December 2013).

Reader, I. (1993) 'Dead to the world: pilgrims in Shikoku', in I. Reader and T. Walter (eds), *Pilgrimage in Popular Culture*, Basingstoke: Macmillan.

RocketNews24 (4 January 2014) 'Train enthusiasts gone wild! Are Japan's train photographers losing their social grace?', available at: http://en.rocketnews24.com/2014/01/04/train-enthusiasts-gone-wild-are-japans-train-photographers-losing-their-social-graces/ (accessed 4 January 2014).

Railway Technical Research Institute and East Japan Railway Culture Foundation (RTRI and EJRCF) (eds) (2001) *Japanese Railway Technology Today*, Tōkyō: East Japan Railway Culture Foundation.

Reischauer, E. O. and Jansen, M. B. (1995) *The Japanese Today: Change and Continuity*, Tōkyō: Charles E. Tuttle Press.

Russell, D. (2004) *Eye of the Whale*, New York: Island Press.

Schencking, J. C. (2013) *The Great Kantō Earthquake and the Chimera of National Reconstruction in Japan*, New York: Columbia University Press.

Schoenbaum, T. J. (2008) *Peace in Northeast Asia: Resolving Japan's Territorial and Maritime Disputes with China, Korea and the Russian Federation*, Cheltenham: Edward Elgar.

Seaton, P. A. (2007) *Japan's Contested War Memories: The 'Memory Rifts' in Historical Consciousness of World War II*, London: Routledge.

Senda, Y. (2013) 'The Japanese family on the brink of change?', available at: www.nippon.com/en/currents/d00095/ (accessed 15 October 2013).

Stockholm International Peace Research Institute (SIPRI) (2014) 'Data by country', available at: http://portal.sipri.org/publications/pages/expenditures/country-search (accessed 6 April 2014).

Tamaru, N. and Reid, D. (1996) *Religion in Japanese Culture*, Tōkyō: Kodansha International.

Tōkyō Metropolitan Government (2013) '*Fujisan ga mieta nissū*', available at: www.taiki.kankyo.metro.tokyo.jp/bunpu1/air1/mt_fuji.htm (accessed 17 July 2013).

Tōkyō Metropolitan Government (2014) 'Overview of Tōkyō', available at: www.metro.tokyo.jp/ENGLISH/PROFILE/overview03.htm (accessed 2 April 2014).

Tokuhiro, Y. (2009) *Marriage in Contemporary Japan*, London: Routledge.

Tyler, E. B. (1873) *Primitive Culture*, London: John Murray.

Uenomura no Chishi Shippitsusha (ed.) (2003) *Uenomurashi (VII) Uenomura no Chishi*, Gunma: Ueno-mura.

UN Data (2014) 'Seats held by women in national parliament, percentage', available at: http://data.un.org/Data.aspx?q=japan&d=MDG&f=seriesRowID%3A557%3BcountryID%3A392 (accessed 10 January 2014).

UNESCO (2013) 'Japan', available at: http://whc.unesco.org/en/statesparties/JP/ (accessed 1 December 2013).

UNESO (2014) 'Lists of intangible cultural heritage and register of best safeguarding practices', available at: www.unesco.org/culture/ich/index.php?pg=00559 (accessed 2 April 2014).

Wattention (2014) '*Omotenashi* – the Heart of Japanese Hospitality', available at: www.wattention.com/archives/omotenashi-the-heart-of-japanese-hospitality/ (accessed 7 March 2014).

Weiner, M. (ed.) (2009) *Japan's Minorities: The Illusion of Homogeneity*, London: Routledge.

The White House (2009) 'Remarks by President Barack Obama at Suntory Hall', available at: www.whitehouse.gov/the-press-office/remarks-president-barack-obama-suntory-hall (accessed 14 November 2009).

World Nuclear Association (2014) 'Nuclear power in Japan', available at: www.world-nuclear.org/info/Country-Profiles/Countries-G-N/Japan/ (accessed 2 April 2014).

Woronoff, J. (1980) *The Coming Social Crisis*, Tōkyō: Yohan.

Yahoo Finance (2013) 'The world's largest automakers', available at: http://finance.yahoo.com/news/world-largest-automakers-222430745.html (accessed 15 September 2013).

Yamanashi Tourism Organisation (2014) 'The nature found in the Aokigahara "sea of trees"', available at: www.yamanashi-kankou.jp/kokuritsukoen/en/miryoku/aokigaharajukai.html (accessed 5 April 2014).

Yano, C. (2011) *Airborne Dreams*, Durham, NC: Duke University Press.

Yoshino, K. (1995) *Cultural Nationalism in Contemporary Japan: A Sociological Enquiry*, London: Routledge.

YouTube (2011a) 'Universal Pictures opening medley (1929–present)', available at: www.youtube.com/watch?v=JtmR4wgE1hM (accessed 1 May 2011).

YouTube (2011b) 'The unluckiest man in the world', available at: www.youtube.com/watch?v=XnTaqBnNLUU (accessed 7 April 2014).

INDEX

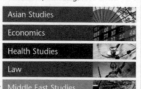